D1576765

Colonial Ireland
in Medieval
English Literature

Colonial Ireland in Medieval English Literature

Elizabeth L. Rambo

SUP

Selinsgrove: Susquehanna University Press
London and Toronto: Associated University Presses

Associated University Presses
440 Forsgate Drive
Cranbury, NJ 08512

Associated University Presses
25 Sicilian Avenue
London WC1A 2QH, England

Associated University Presses
P.O. Box 338, Port Credit
Mississauga, Ontario
Canada L5G 4L8

The paper used in this publication meets the requirements
of the American National Standard for Permanence of Paper
for Printed Library Materials Z39.48-1984.

Library of Congress Cataloging-in-Publication Data

Rambo, Elizabeth L., 1954–
    Colonial Ireland in medieval English literature / Elizabeth L. Rambo.
        p.   cm.
    Based on the author's thesis (Ph.D., University of North Carolina at Chapel Hill).
    Includes bibliographical references and index.
    ISBN 0-945636-61-X (alk. paper)
    1. English literature—Middle English, 1100–1500—History and criticism.   2. English literature—Irish influences.   3. Colonies in literature.   4. Ireland—In literature.   I. Title.
PR128.R36   1994
820.9'32415'0902—dc20   93-46784
                                                                CIP

To my parents,
V. Birch Rambo, M.D., and Margaret Gordon Rambo

To my grandmother, Louise Birch Rambo,
and in memory of my grandfather,
Victor C. Rambo, M.D., 1894–1987

Contents

Acknowledgments

Portions of this work were presented at the Medieval Association of the Pacific Annual Meeting, February 1992. Thanks to the Institute for the Arts and Humanities of the College of Arts and Sciences, University of North Carolina at Chapel Hill. Thanks to Professor Patrick P. O'Neill, University of North Carolina at Chapel Hill, who oversaw the earlier drafts of this book as my dissertation director. Others who read it and suggested valuable revisions and corrections include University of North Carolina professors Connie C. Eble, Edward D. Kennedy, Theodore H. Leinbaugh, and Joseph S. Wittig. Any errors or inaccuracies are, of course, my own. Thanks to the Research and Development Committee of Biola University for providing financial support for the completion of this project. I'm also grateful to Professor Virginia Doland of Biola University for her help as I prepared the manuscript for publication. And always, thanks to my husband, James W. Pence, III.

Copyright Permissions

Thanks to the following authors, editors, and publishers for permission to quote passages from their works:

Bede's Ecclesiastical History of the English People, edited and translated by Bertram Colgrave and R. A. B. Mynors. © 1969 Oxford University Press. Used by permission of Oxford University Press.

Capgrave, John, *Capgrave's Abbreuiacion of Cronicles,* edited by Peter J. Lucas. © 1983 Oxford University Press. Used by permission of The Council of the Early English Text Society.

Chestre, Thomas, *Sir Launfal,* edited by A. J. Bliss. Nelson: Medieval & Renaissance Library (1960). © 1960 Thomas Nelson & Sons Ltd. Used by permission.

Collis, Louise, *Memoirs of a Medieval Woman: The Life of Margery Kempe.* © 1964 by Louise Collis. Used by permission of the author.

Gerald of Wales, *The History and Topography of Ireland,* translated by

10 ACKNOWLEDGMENTS

John O'Meara (Penguin Classics, 1982), © 1951, 1982 by John J. O'Meara. Used by permission.

Kane, George and E. Talbot Donaldson, eds., *Piers Plowman: The B Version,* by William Langland. © 1975 by George Kane and E. Talbot Donaldson. Used by the kind permission of Professor Kane.

Kempe, Margery. *The Book of Margery Kempe,* edited by Sanford Brown Meech and Hope Emily Allen. © 1940 Oxford University Press. Used by permission of The Council of the Early English Text Society.

Kenney, James F. *The Sources for the Early History of Ireland,* Vol. 1: Ecclesiastical. 1929. Revised by Ludwig Bieler, 1966; rpt. Dublin: Pádraic Ó Táilliúir, 1979. © 1979 Hippocrene Books, Inc. Used by permission.

King Horn, edited by Rosamund Allen. © 1984 by Rosamund Allen. Used by permission.

Laʒamon, *Brut,* edited by G. L. Brook and R. F. Leslie. © 1963, 1969 Oxford University Press. Used by permission of The Council of the Early English Text Society.

Lybeaus Desconus, edited by M. Mills. © 1969 Oxford University Press. Used by permission of The Council of the Early English Text Society.

Malory, Thomas, *Works,* edited by Eugène Vinaver. © 1978 Oxford University Press. Used by permission of Oxford University Press.

Nennius, *British History and The Welsh Annals.* Reproduced by kind permission from the Arthurian Period Sources volume NENNIUS (ed. and trans. by Dr. John Morris), published in 1980 by Phillimore & Co., Ltd., Shopwyke Manor Barn, Chichester, West Sussex, England.

Of Arthoure and of Merlin, edited by O. D. Macrae-Gibson. © 1973, 1979 Oxford University Press. Used by permission of The Council of the Early English Text Society.

Otway-Ruthven, A. J., *A History of Medieval Ireland,* 2d ed. © A. J. Otway-Ruthven, 1967. Used by permission from A & C Black (Publishers) Ltd., Howard Road, Eaton Socon, Huntingdon, Cambs PE19 3EZ, United Kingdom.

The Owl and the Nightingale, edited by E. G. Stanley. Nelson: Medieval & Renaissance Library (1960). © 1960 Thomas Nelson & Sons Ltd. Used by permission.

Robinson, F. N. (Editor), *The Works of Geoffrey Chaucer.* © 1957 by Houghton Mifflin Company. Used with permission.

The South English Legendary, Vol. 1, edited by Charlotte D'Evelyn and Arna J. Mill. © 1956 Oxford University Press. Used by permission of The Council of the Early English Text Society.

Watt, J. A., *The Church and the Two Nations in Medieval Ireland.* © 1970 by J. A. Watt. Used by permission of the author.

Colonial Ireland
in Medieval
English Literature

1

Introduction

Little has been written about England's attitudes toward Ireland before the sixteenth century, except from historical and political perspectives, although there are numerous studies of English-Irish relations in the sixteenth century and beyond. Perhaps the best known, David Beers Quin's *The Elizabethans and the Irish,* draws on a wide variety of contemporary accounts, government documents, poetry, and drama, to present a vivid picture of two cultures in conflict.[1] The writer of such a work is aided by two factors. First, England's involvement in Irish affairs increases markedly beginning in the sixteenth century. And second, because of this increased involvement, and due to the simple fact that more manuscripts and printed works of all kinds from this period and later are still extant, the writer's primary resources are much greater than those available for the medieval period.

For the medieval period, however, most of the existing studies[2] are based primarily upon historical sources such as chronicles, annals, and government documents. Even so, as Quin acknowledged, "How and out of what materials England invented her cultural nationalism [with regard to Ireland] has been very inadequately explored by her historians."[3] Until quite recently, E. D. Snyder's article, "The Wild Irish: A Study of Some English Satires Against the Irish, Scots, and Welsh" (1920), was the only previous attempt to examine evidence concerning English attitudes toward Ireland and the Irish in literary sources, and since Snyder surveyed English literature from the Middle Ages through the nineteenth century, unfortunately, he was able to treat the literature of any particular period only superficially.[4] Snyder's thesis is that the English have generally viewed all the Celtic races—Irish, Scots, and Welsh—as simply barbaric. Though this may well represent a general tendency on the part of the English, it seems unlikely that it could be the whole picture, especially during the early years of English involvement in Irish affairs, that is, from 1170 through the

the fifteenth century. F. X. Martin's 1985 address, "The Image of the Irish—Medieval and Modern—Continuity and Change," takes a more balanced approach, by drawing on Latin religious and historical sources from England and the Continent, but again, covers more than twelve centuries in a mere eighteen pages.[5] Therefore, a study focusing on ways in which Middle English literature reflects English attitudes toward Ireland and the Irish seemed particularly worthwhile because it was during this time that England began to establish her claim to rule Ireland, following her initial conquest of portions of the island in the late twelfth century. I shall investigate, first, various ways in which Middle English literary references to Ireland and the Irish during the first three centuries of England's colonial presence in the island reflect English knowledge of, and attitudes toward, Ireland and her people. In addition, I shall consider to what extent these references may have influenced the views of English readers, especially educated laypersons. As Walter Ullmann has argued, "Fiction and legend having been enshrined in 'history', tend to become tradition which then begins to operate as a powerfully stimulating and generating factor of the historical process itself."[6]

The focus on Middle English texts is based on the hypothesis that, with the rise of secular literacy during this period, vernacular texts are most likely to have influenced and reflected the views of educated laypersons, not just the clerical elite. In England (and throughout Western Europe) during the twelfth and thirteenth centuries, the Church's role in education increased greatly. In England, the founding of universities and the growing importance of written records in all walks of life meant that "even those who had no immediate practical need to do so began to take more interest in books."[7] Early literacy among the upper classes involved primarily Latin and French, but English continued to be the first language of laypersons in the middle and lower classes everywhere, and especially in works intended to be read aloud or performed, such as lyrics and carols, sermons and devotional works, and romances.[8]

By the latter half of the fourteenth century, English had established itself even among the nobility.[9] Even earlier, however, there had been a "decline of French in aristocratic circles."[10] Also, during this time, grammar schools were established in order to teach reading and writing to "the humbler members of society,"[11] and although the curriculum was Latin grammar and composition, instruction was in English.[12]

English nationalism was another factor in the growing acceptance and interest in the English language. For example, in 1377,

Chancellor Robert Ashton warned Parliament of the possibility of war with France, saying that the French, added to England's other enemies, "make us surrounded on all sides so that [they] can destroy our lord the king and his realm of England, and *drive out the English language*" (italics mine).[13]

The writing of history was "no longer restricted to monastic authors or foundations,"[14] and new chronicles were written and read by secular clerks and laypersons. Other genres, such as devotional works, romance, and estates satire, also reached a wider readership, including "a large number of the urban 'middle class'."[15] *Piers Plowman,* for example, a complex and evidently widely read poem, would have reached an audience of both laypersons and ecclesiastics whose "customary activities involve[d] them in counsel, policy, education, administration, pastoral care— those tasks and offices where spiritual and temporal governance meet."[16] It is not unreasonable to argue, as Janet Coleman does, that during the fourteenth century "English verse and prose increasingly became widespread vehicles of education and incitement to change as well as 'mirrors of contemporary man,'"[17] and this trend continues to grow in the fifteenth century as English increasingly replaces both French and Latin in all sectors of society.

Methodology

The study divides the Middle English literature that contains references to Ireland and the Irish into four broad classes (chronicles, romances, and hagiography and other religious writings), ordering works in each class more or less chronologically, and examines references to Ireland and the Irish in each work in light of the different origins and purposes of the genres. This organization seemed more practical than a primarily chronological approach, given the difficulty of dating most Middle English texts and manuscripts. A plan based on classifying positive and negative references seemed oversimplified, and would have required some kind of subclassification as well, such as the generic one.

In analyzing this material, I have taken two different approaches. First, I have tried to identify, wherever possible, Irish sources and analogues of various motifs, especially in dealing with romances and saints' lives, in order to consider the possibility that some Middle English writers may have drawn upon Irish material (consciously or unconsciously), and to examine some possible routes for the transmission of such materials. If it can be shown that writers were aware of their Irish sources, this may tell us something about English knowledge of, and attitudes toward, Ireland and the Irish. On the other hand, if borrowings seem unconscious, they reveal little about English views, though one may still speculate about possible routes of transmission.

Second, I have considered the extent to which any particular reference to Ireland or the Irish might have reflected the views of its writer, and what influence it may have had upon readers of the text. The first question involves such complex issues as the role of a translator in adding to or altering his original, and the difficult to impossible task of guessing whether any reference reflects only the view of its writer, or whether the writer is recording an opinion commonly held by his community. The second question depends upon how well-known or influential any given work may have been, based upon the number of extant manuscripts and the number of times other works use the first as a source, though any answer to this question can rarely be more than speculative, since countless medieval manuscripts are lost to us.

Hiberno-English texts, that is, Middle English texts originally written in the English colonies in Ireland, are for the most part removed from the discussion, on the assumption that the attitudes and concerns of English people living in Ireland (for generations, in many cases) are likely to have been different from those of residents in England—more informed, perhaps, if often less sympathetic. The Hiberno-English, like other march-dwelling people, came to view themselves (and to be viewed by others) as a "middle nation," neither English nor Irish, but with characteristics of both, according to the historian James Lydon.[18] This group of people became aware of their distinction as early as the twelfth century, and continued to be classified as such as late as 1600.[19] In a few instances, Hiberno-English sources may be cited to further support evidence found in English texts.[20]

Contemporary Latin works of English provenance are discussed where they provide supporting evidence and to place hagiographic, homiletic, and historical materials in context. Also, in many cases, the Middle English works are translated from Latin sources and the relationship between original and translation may be informative. For example, it would be impossible to discuss English ideas about Ireland and the Irish without reference to Giraldus Cambrensis's late twelfth-century *Historia et Topographia Hibernica* and *Expugnatio Hibernica,* which for centuries were the main sources of firsthand information on Ireland for English chroniclers. One must also remember that most Middle English saints' lives were first translated from Latin *vitae,* some of which were of Irish origin.

Historical Background: English-Irish Relations, 1166–1500[21]

England's political involvement with Ireland begins in the midtwelfth century. Prior to that time, with the exception of the Hiberno-Norse Viking raiders on England (the "Scots" of the ninth through the eleventh centuries), relatively cordial religious and mercantile relations had been the main avenues of interisland communications. The Norman Conquest of England may have disrupted these exchanges, to some extent, with the changing adminstrations in state and church, but in any case, the new rulers of England were much too busy establishing themselves to pay much attention to the neighboring island. One question to be considered is whether subsequent events that drew English political attention to Ireland, affected English attitudes toward Ireland generally, and if so, to what extent are these changes reflected in literary sources?[22]

In 1166, Dermot MacMurrough (Diarmait Mac Murchada), king of Leinster, fled Ireland and landed in Bristol, seeking help in his efforts to regain his territory, which he had lost to his enemies Rory O'Connor (Toirrdelbach Ua Conchobair) and Tighernan O'Rourke (Ua Ruairc). The hostility between these two and MacMurrough was of long standing, but Dermot had earned O'Rourke's lasting hatred by abducting his wife, Devorgilla (Derbforgaill), in 1152, while O'Rourke was away fighting another king. This action, more politically than romantically motivated, at least on Dermot's part, was perhaps only "another unfortunate factor,"[23] for there were "far bigger issues at stake."[24]

From Bristol, Dermot went on to find Henry II in Aquitaine, where Henry "was fully occupied with his own affairs," according to A. J. Otway-Ruthven,

> but he received Dermot kindly, took homage and fealty from him, promised him help, and gave him letters authorizing his subjects to give him aid as "our vassal and liegeman" in recovering his kingdom. He sent orders to fitz Harding at Bristol to provide for Dermot, and then no doubt dismissed him from his mind.[25]

Thus began the English conquest of Ireland.

Dermot found his Norman ally in Richard fitz Gilbert de Clare, lord of Strigoil and earl of Pembroke, called "Strongbow," though it would be three years before his promised aid actually materialized. In 1170, Norman-Welsh mercenary troops under Strongbow went to Ireland and, with their superior arms and training, quickly overcame resistance in Leinster. In return for this support, Dermot named Strongbow as his heir; he died in 1171, leaving Strongbow and his relatively small band of soldiers more or less stranded. Strongbow had little hope for reinforcements from England because by this time, ironically, Henry II had changed his mind about England's involvement with Ireland.

> Immediately before [Strongbow's] embarkation in 1170, when it was already too late to draw back, messengers from Henry had arrived to forbid the expedition, and already before Dermot's death the king had ordered all his subjects in Ireland to return home before Easter on pain of forfeiture and perpetual banishment, and had forbidden exports to Ireland.[26]

In the end, it seems, Henry II intervened in Ireland at the request of the Irish themselves, who wanted Strongbow out. As Otway-Ruthven points out, "Clearly Henry could not afford to let Strongbow establish himself as an independent ruler, and we need not suppose that he was unwilling to acquire fresh lands for himself, especially if he had been given reason to think that the Irish might welcome him."[27] When Henry himself visited Ireland (1171–72), he received oaths of fealty from a number of Irish princes, and the wholehearted support of the Irish church. The twelfth century was a time of great reforms in the Irish church, and Henry arrived not long after the council of Cashel, where the Irish bishops had "prepared a statement of what Giraldus describes as 'the enormous offences and foul lives of the people of that land'. . . . Each bishop further gave Henry letters under his seal confirming his submission, and these were subsequently sent to the pope."[28]

This was Henry's first and last visit to Ireland, but it was not enough to establish his authority permanently over the whole territory. Years of conflict among the Irish chieftains followed. In 1177, Henry named his son, John, lord of Ireland, but it was not until 1185 that Prince John could lead a second invasion force into Ireland, this time with the intention of fully establishing English rule there. Otway-Ruthven writes, "John's expedition was prepared with great care, but . . . the character of the new lord of Ireland ensured that its purely political effects should be unfortunate."[29]

Among John's followers was the Norman-Welsh cleric Giraldus Cambrensis, who described John's arrival in Waterford as follows:

> [T]here met him at Waterford a great many of the Irish of the better class in those parts; men who, having been hitherto loyal to the English and disposed to be peaceable, came to congratulate him as their new lord, and receive him with the kiss of peace. But our newcomers and Normans not only treated them with contempt and derision, but even rudely pulled them by their beards, which the Irishmen wore full and long, according to the custom of their country.[30]

John and his men seem to have continued as they had begun, so that by the time they left Ireland, eight months later, they had alienated those Irish who supported English rule, several Irish rulers who had originally intended to submit to England for the first time, and even the church.[31] Fortunately, the men he left behind him to rule were more temperate and diplomatic, and were able to regain, literally and figuratively, some of the ground John had lost. One of them was Theobald Walter, founder of the Butler family of Ormonde, to whom John granted large tracts of land in what are now the Irish counties of Clare, Offaly, Tipperary, and Limerick.

John returned to Ireland as king in 1210 with his feudal levy and Flemish mercenaries,[32] to take back lands held by the de Lacy family. He was more successful this time, not only obtaining the de Lacy's surrender, but also receiving oaths of fealty from twenty Irish kings, according to the chronicler Roger of Wendover.[33] Concerning John's second expedition and its results, Otway-Ruthven writes:

> All this adds up to a considerable achievement, but it was to be suggested in the next reign that John had done a good deal more. According to Henry III
>> he caused to be made and to be sworn to by the magnates of Ireland [a charter] concerning the observance of the laws and customs of England in Ireland . . . the laws and customs of the realm of England which the lord king John our father of happy memory with the common consent of all men of Ireland ordained to be kept in that land.
> No such charter as this writ refers to has survived, but the statement is so precise that it is impossible to doubt that one existed.[34]

Whether such a charter indeed had "the common consent of all men of Ireland," is open to question, however.

One event in Ireland that received considerable attention in England was the death of Richard Marshal in 1234. Richard's family had long been loyal supporters of England in Ireland, but a dispute over the Marshal holdings in France led to a conflict between Richard and Henry III. Richard was attacked in Ireland while attempting to negotiate a truce with Henry, and died two weeks later of his wounds. According to English chronicles, he was murdered by his own Irish vassals, "but there is no other evidence for this," according to Otway-Ruthven.[35] Rather, evidence exists that Richard's assassination was condoned (if not initiated) by Henry III and carried out by Englishmen.[36] Also during the thirteenth century, notes F. X. Martin, Irish students at Oxford "took a prominent part" in "the much publicised student riots. . . . Attention was not drawn to the fact that one of the most influential professors instructing Thomas Aquinas at Naples was Peter of Ireland."[37]

In 1315, Edward Bruce of Scotland, brother of Robert Bruce, landed in Ireland, about a year after Robert's decisive defeat of the English under Edward II at Bannockburn. Some political, mercantile, and cultural connections had long existed between Scotland and Ireland, and at this time, a Scottish invasion of Ireland would serve three purposes for the Scots: it would distract the English from their war with Scotland, shut off an important source of English mercenary troops, and Ireland could become Edward's territory under Robert, thus preventing Edward from causing trouble in Scotland.[38] The native Irish at first supported him, and he overcame a great part of Ulster and Meath. During this time, Donnell O'Neill, calling himself "king of Ulster and true heir by hereditary right of all Ireland,"[39] sent the pope the document called "the remonstrance of the Irish princes," in which he protested that the English colonists were treating the Irish people and church shamefully:

He alleged that the churches had been deprived of half their possessions; he complained bitterly that the Irish were not allowed the benefits of English law; he complained of the statute [of Kilkenny] that no mere Irishman should be admitted into a religious order among the English . . . and alleged that the English said it was no worse to kill an Irishman than a brute beast: Friar Simon, brother of the bishop of Connor, had expressly said before Edward Bruce that it was no sin to kill an Irishman, and if he did so himself he would nonetheless celebrate mass. Two years earlier many of the Irish had sent letters to the king [of England], offering to hold their lands immediately of him, but had had no reply: they had called on Bruce to aid them, and O'Neill had granted him all his right in the kingdom by his letters patent.[40]

Internal problems in England prevented Edward II from dealing effectively with the Scots in Ireland until 1318, when English troops finally defeated the Scots and killed Edward Bruce. With the removal of Bruce and the Scots, the Irish seem to have been as relieved as the English, despite O'Neill's earlier "remonstrance." Their annals, "with striking unanimity,"[41] call Bruce

> the common ruin of the Gaels and Galls of Ireland . . . never was there a better deed done for the Irish than this, since the beginning of the world and the banishing of the Fomorians from Ireland. For in this Bruce's time, for three years and a half, falsehood and famine and homicide filled the country, and undoubtedly men ate each other in Ireland.[42]

Ireland continued to be a source of men, revenues, and supplies for England's wars with Scotland and France over the next twenty years.[43] However, England seems to have neglected internal affairs among the Irish and Hiberno-English colonists, and by 1341, the Irish (i.e., Hiberno-English) parliament sent petitions to King Edward III asking him to deal with various forms of official corruption and injustice in the English territories. Edward took some steps to address these problems, but over the next several years the general disorder among the English colonists gave opportunities to a number of Irish chieftains to attack English lands.[44] Added to this unrest was the Black Death, which reached Ireland in 1348 and broke out at intervals during the remainder of the fourteenth century, with a further epidemic recorded in January 1425.[45] Ireland, England, and indeed all of Europe were demoralized by this plague.

In 1366, as part of English efforts to control their Irish territory, an Irish Parliament passed the Statutes of Kilkenny, which many historians have considered "a kind of watershed in the history of the English colony in Ireland," although, according to Otway-Ruthven, they merely codified principles which in many cases had long been in practice.[46] The statutes seem to have been prompted by fears that the Hiberno-English were "going native," as stated in the preamble.

> [A]t the conquest of the land of Ireland and long after the English of the said land used the English language, dress, and manner of riding, and they and their subjects called betaghs were governed by English law . . . and now many English of the said land, forsaking the English language, fashion, manner of riding, laws and usages, live and govern themselves by the manners, fashion, and language of the Irish enemies,

and have made divers marriages and alliances between themselves and the Irish enemies, by which the said land and its liege people, the English language, the allegiance due to our lord the king, and the English laws are put in subjection and decayed, and the Irish enemies raised up and relieved contrary to reason.[47]

The statutes prohibited any family alliance between Irish and English; required that both English and native Irish in English territory must speak only English; refused entry to cathedrals and churches or to religious orders by Irishmen; and "forbade Irish minstrels to come among the English or be received by them, 'since they spy out their secrets, whereby great evils have often happened.'"[48] They also enacted a variety of measures for colonial defense and civil peace-keeping, for example, "If any Englishman breaks a truce or peace . . . between English and Irish he is responsible for the damages resulting, and shall make fine at the king's will. No Englishman shall stir up war against others on pain of life and limb and forfeiture of lands."[49]

General unrest continued in Ireland, despite the Statutes of Kilkenny and other measures taken by the Hiberno-English rulers. Conflicts among various Irish clans and between the Irish and Hiberno-English erupted again and again, while England dealt with her own political problems between the death of Edward III and the accession of Richard II in 1389. It was not until 1394 that Richard was able to turn his attention to his Irish territory.

In June of 1394, Richard proclaimed

> that all men born in Ireland should return there immediately, as he had taken the firm resolve shortly to go there in person, 'in certain hope . . . of better and more prosperously ruling the land and people there than heretofore used to be done.'[56]

In October, he landed at Waterford with an army estimated at eight to ten thousand men,[51] including both English and Irish forces, and within a year had obtained submission from "practically every important chief in Ireland."[52] In a letter to his regent and council, Richard identified three types of men in Ireland:

> wild Irish, our enemies, Irish rebels, and obedient English . . . the said Irish rebels are rebels only because of grievances and wrongs done to them on one side, and lack of remedy on the other. If they are not wisely treated and put in good hope of grace they will probably join our enemies.[53]

This, Richard's first expedition, was "up to a point, a remarkable success,"[54] but there was still the problem of Hiberno-English rebels, and new disputes arose over territory claimed by both English and Irish. In 1397, Richard declared his intention to return to Ireland to deal with these new troubles, and in 1399, evidently believing that things were well under control in England, he returned to Ireland. The enormous taxes and levies required for this expedition made it and the king not so popular as in 1394. Henry of Lancaster took advantage of Richard's absence and the discontent of the English people to return from exile. Richard came back from Ireland to face Henry, but by September 1399, Henry IV was king of England.

Otway-Ruthven writes, "With the departure of Richard and his army, . . . Ireland was left in a state of confusion . . . but Ireland was the least of the problems which faced Henry IV."[55] Throughout the first half of the fifteenth century, a series of more or less incompetent and tyrannical deputies and lords lieutenant plundered the island for its meager revenues, and did little or nothing to calm the various conflicts among the Irish and Hiberno-English, but rather stirred things up.[56]

During the Wars of the Roses, Ireland became a base for Yorkist operations under Richard, Duke of York. He had been appointed lieutenant by Henry VI in 1447, and reappointed in 1457. In 1460, Richard convened an Irish parliament which passed acts that strengthened his security in Ireland.

> It had been made treasonable to attack him in any way; it had been made impossible for his enemies in England to proceed against any of his supporters in Ireland; he had created a force of archers for himself . . . ; and . . . had done something to provide . . . funds.[57]

Later that year, Richard took his Irish forces to England, reached London, and claimed the Crown by right of inheritance. However, Parliament did not accept him, but reached a compromise whereby Henry VI would retain the crown for life, with York and his heirs to inherit. Later this plan was defeated along with Henry VI in 1461, when Richard's son Edward overcame the Lancastrians to become Edward IV. Henry and his queen escaped to Scotland.

While the Yorkists were engaged in consolidating their position in England, certain Hiberno-English nobles, primarily the lords of Kildare and the Butlers of Ormond, were establishing their own power base in Ireland. In 1479, Richard III began negotiating with Kildare, but before much progress could be made (as Otway-Ruthven puts it), "in England the disaffection which had existed throughout Richard's reign was mounting, while Henry Tudor, the last, though doubtful, heir of the Lancastrians, was preparing an invasion, supported by France."[58] In 1485, Henry overthrew Richard and was crowned Henry VII.

In Ireland, however, there was still support for the York faction, and in 1487 a Yorkist pretender to the throne, one Lambert Simnel, masquerading as Edward, earl of Warwick, was crowned Edward VI in Dublin. In June an army of the Hiberno-English, with a native Irish force and five-thousand German mercenaries, attacked England, where they were soon defeated and Simnel was captured, but in Ireland Kildare and his supporters did not surrender until the end of the year.[59] In 1491, another Yorkist pretender, Perkin Warbeck, raised considerable support in Ireland from Kildare, Desmond, and others. But finally, in 1494, Kildare and other Irish nobles who had supported Warbeck came to England and gave Henry VII their fealty.

Nevertheless, dissension and intrigues continued in Ireland, and finally the earl of Ormond, another of the most powerful Hiberno-English nobles, accused Kildare of conspiring against the English king's deputy. Kildare was arrested and imprisoned in the Tower in 1495. During this time, an Irish parliament under Henry's deputy, Poynings, had passed acts

> which explicitly subordinated the parliament of Ireland to the English council. . . . Though the disorders of Ireland made it necessary to send Kildare back as deputy in 1496, Poynings' acts mark a clear watershed between medieval Ireland and the Tudor period.[60]

To sum up the first three centuries of English rule in Ireland (which is not to say that the English ruled all Ireland by any means, for they had merely established a foothold): In the early years, Ireland offered new feudal territories to be parceled out to Norman nobles. After the thirteenth century, for the most part, England found Ireland a convenient source of revenue and troops, except during the brief tenure of Edward Bruce during the Scots' war against England in the early fourteenth century. Ireland also became a useful place of exile for those out of favor at court, and an equally useful headquarters for launching rebellions against the Crown. Except for these rebellions and a few other crises, such as internal conflicts among the Irish and Hiberno-English, and concern over whether the Hiberno-English families were becoming too Hibernicized, the English government generally ignored Ireland during the late medieval period.

2

Ireland in Middle English Chronicles and Historical Poems

We cannot examine Middle English vernacular chronicles without considering some of the earlier or contemporary Latin chronicles which were, in many cases, their sources. There are dozens of medieval Latin chronicles, mostly monastic in origin, but four which turn up more frequently than any others as sources for Middle English chronicles which treat of Irish affairs (and for later Latin chronicles) are Bede's *Historia Ecclesiastica Gentis Anglorum* (ca. 731), Geoffrey of Monmouth's *Historia Regum Britanniae* (ca. 1136), and Giraldus Cambrensis's *Historia et Topographia Hibernica* (1188) and *Expugnatio Hibernica* (1189).[1] A fifth is Ranulph Higden's *Polychronicon* (1327–52) which was immensely popular both in Latin and in English translations, including one by John Trevisa (1387)[2] and two late fifteenth-century printed editions by Caxton (1482) and de Worde (1495).[3] Higden drew his material from a wide variety of sources, including the four just named and many others, such as William of Malmesbury's *De Gestis Regum Anglorum* (ca. 1142), and Matthew Paris's *Chronica Maiora* (late thirteenth/early fourteenth century).[4] These and other Latin chronicles continued to be read in the original during the medieval period and, except for the *Polychronicon,*[5] were apparently never translated into Middle English, though portions might be summarized, paraphrased, or translated verbatim, and then inserted into vernacular works. In general, I shall limit my reference to Latin chronicles to the five that seem to dominate as sources of significant passages concerning Ireland and the Irish in Middle English chronicles.

The Middle English chronicles that refer to Ireland and the Irish briefly or at length, are as follows: Laȝamon, *Brut* (ca. 1225); Robert of Gloucester, *Metrical Chronicle* (late thirteenth century; Manuscript 1320–30), and a later prose paraphrase of the same chronicle (fifteenth century); the anonymous *Prose Brut* (1350–80/

1400); Robert Mannyng of Brunne, *The Story of England* (1338); John Trevisa's translation of Ranulph Higden's *Polychronicon* (late fourteenth century), and an anonymous fifteenth-century translation (Manuscript Harley 2261); John Capgrave, *Abbreuiacion of Cronicles* (ca. 1462–3); and William Caxton's *Chronicles of England* and his encyclopedia, the *Mirrour of the World* (both late fifteenth century).[6]

Who wrote historical works in the Middle English period, and who read them? Before the twelfth century, chronicles had been primarily the work of monastic writers, producing histories or annals for their own houses. From the twelfth century onward, chronicles are written by secular clergy as well, who often dedicated them to noble patrons and perhaps looked for a wider audience as well. Geoffrey of Monmouth, for example, may have been a canon of St. George's College in Oxford,[7] and dedicated his *Historia Regum Britanniae* to Robert, earl of Gloucester, the natural son of Henry I, and to Waleran, count of Mellent, son of Robert de Beaumont. Giraldus Cambrensis addressed the *Historia et Topographia Hibernica* to Henry II. In the thirteenth and fourteenth centuries, secular literacy became more common, at least among the upper classes and probably among the growing bourgeoisie as well; educated persons were often trilingual. Laypersons, in addition to secular clerics, began to write or compile chronicles in Latin, English, and French (though French was rarely used after the fourteenth century). "Such chronicles," writes Janet Coleman in *Medieval Writers and Readers: 1350–1400,* "were no longer restricted to monastic authors or foundations: seculars read and possessed them—Thomas, Duke of Gloucester's library inventory listed nine of them."[8]

England's Right to Rule Ireland

In comparing pre and postconquest English chronicles, one detects a definite change of attitude toward Ireland and the Irish after the Norman Conquest. The British and Anglo-Saxon historical works that we know of—Gildas's *De Excidio Britanniae* (ca. 540),[9] Bede's *Historia Ecclesiastica Gentis Anglorum* (731), and Nennius's *Historia Brittonum et Annales Cambriae* (ca. 820)—show little interest in English political power over Ireland. This is not to imply that the preconquest British and Anglo-Saxon chroniclers were favorably disposed toward the Irish, but they seem more concerned about the Irish raiding England, rather than the other way around. Gildas has nothing good to say about the "Scoti" (as they were known then), calling them "exceedingly savage" in their alliance with the Picts against the British after the Romans' withdrawal.[10] He compares them to "greedy wolves, rabid with extreme hunger, who, dry-mouthed, leap over into the sheepfold when the shepherd is away."[11]

Bede is gentler with the Irish than most English or Anglo-Norman chroniclers, perhaps because his is an "ecclesiastical history" and he must give credit to Irish missionaries such as Columba and Aidan. After a very pleasant description of Ireland itself (19–20), he then takes the post-Roman history of Britain almost verbatim from Gildas, but omitting the lurid descriptions of the Irish invaders (40–44), though he does term them "extremely fierce" (40). Bede mentions with approval the Irish tradition of scholarship and their hospitality to English monks (312), and their exemplary asceticism (308–10, 478–80). Nevertheless, throughout his history, he goes into much disapproving detail concerning the Easter controversy, since in his view the Irish were quite wrong in refusing for so long to accept Rome's reckoning of the date of Easter.

Nennius, although he records the Irish attacks against Britain, generally maintains a more objective tone and includes few inflammatory details or figures of speech such as those found in Gildas. For example, in recording the distressing period following the withdrawal of Roman troops, he writes simply, "Vortigern ruled in Britain, and during his rule in Britain he was under pressure, from fear of the Picts and the Irish, and of a Roman invasion, and, not least, from dread of Ambrosius."[12] He spends much more time on the career of St. Patrick (33–35). (It is worth noting that Nennius was probably Welsh, and Wales generally remained on good terms with Ireland.) The *Anglo-Saxon Chronicle* also seems fairly objective in its treatment of Ireland.[13]

One of the most significant differences between pre- and post-conquest historical works, is in the story of how Ireland was first settled. The earliest version is in Bede's *Historia Ecclesiastica*.

After [the Britons] had got possesion of the greater part of the island [of Britain], beginning from the south, it is related that the Pictish race from Scythia sailed out into the ocean in a few warships and were carried by the wind beyond the furthest bounds of Britain, reaching Ireland and landing on its northern shores. There they found the Irish race and asked permission to settle among them but their request was refused. (17–19)

In this version, the Scots (i.e., Irish) have already settled in Ireland (no mention of how they got there) and they send the Picts to northern Britain. Then, according to Bede, the Picts obtain wives from the Scots, on the condition that they shall determine royal descent through the female line, and still later, a group of Scots also settle in northern Britain under "Reuda," and maintain a separate colony (19).

Nennius *(Historia Britonum),* in accounts that seem to be drawn more or less from Irish sources,[14] says that the Irish came originally from Spain. I include this long passage in order to highlight the few elements of it that appear in later, postconquest versions:

> Partholon came first with a thousand, men and women, and they grew until they were four thousand, and plague came upon them, and in one week they all died, and there remained not a one of them. Nemet, son of Agnoman, came second to Ireland, and is said to have sailed over the sea for a year and a half, and then made port in Ireland, by shipwreck, and stayed there many years, and set sail again with his people, and returned to Spain. Later, three sons of a warrior in Spain came with thirty keels between them, and thirty wives in each keel, and stayed there for the space of a year. Later, they saw a glass tower in the midst of the sea, and saw men upon the tower, and sought to speak with them, but they never replied; and in the one year they made haste to attack the tower, with all their keels and all their women, except one keel, that was shipwrecked, in which were thirty men and as many women. The other ships sailed to attack the tower, and when they all disembarked on the shore that was around the tower, the sea overwhelmed them, and they were drowned, and no one of them escaped; and from the crew of that one ship that was left behind because of the shipwreck all Ireland was filled, to the present day; and afterwards they came over gradually from Spain, and held many districts. (20)

Noting that "there is . . . nothing certain about the history of the Irish" (20), Nennius also includes "what the Irish scholars have told me" (21), the story that the Irish came from Egypt (descendants of a Scythian and his Egyptian wife "Scotta") to Spain, then to Dal Riada in northwestern Britain, and finally to Ireland "in the Fourth Age" (21).

One common element of both Bede's and Nennius's tales is the fact that the Britons play no part in the settlement of Ireland, though they do have dealings with the Picts in Britain. And although there are some common motifs in both tales which also appear in chronicles written after the Norman Conquest—Scythia, Spain, a journey by ship, a bargain between the Picts and Scots (Irish)—neither of these passages appears to be a primary source for any postconquest chronicle, Latin or English.

Instead, the story of the settlement of Ireland one finds versions of in later chronicles goes like this: a British king (Gurguint or Gurguntius, though the prose *Brut* names him "Corinbatrus"), returning by sea from a victory in the north, encounters a number of ships (sometimes given as thirty, as in Nennius) full of men and women. Their leader (named "Partholoim" [Geoffrey of Monmouth],[15] "Pantolaus" [Laʒamon], "Partalius" [Manning], "Bartholomewe" [Higden/Trevisa], or "Irlanyal" [Gloucester]) explains that they are exiles from Spain (or Egypt, via Spain [Laʒamon, Gloucester]) and they are looking for a place to settle. (The name of the leader and the Spanish origin of the exiles are the only details traceable to the earliest British source, Nennius.) Gurguint sends them to Ireland, which is usually described as having been uninhabited at the time.

The earliest version of this tale is found in Geoffrey of Monmouth's *Historia Regum Britanniae,* probably a source for most of the later chronicles—Giraldus's *Topographia Hibernica* (1188) and *Expugnatio Hibernica;* Laʒamon's *Brut* (ca. 1225, through Wace); the *Metrical Chronicle* of Robert of Gloucester (earliest MS. dated 1320–30); the *Story of England* by Robert Mannyng of Brunne (1338); the prose *Brut* (midfourteenth century); and Trevisa's translation of Ranulph Higden's *Polychronicon* (fifteenth century, taken from Giraldus). The arrival of the Picts in Scotland (from Scythia, according to Gloucester) and their bargain with the Irish appears in Geoffrey of Monmouth, Laʒamon, Gloucester, and Manning and generally follows Bede's version.

In the postconquest version of the settlement of Ireland, the land is granted to the Spanish exiles by a British king, in contrast to the preconquest version, in which they discover and settle Ireland on their own, either by design or by chance (Nennius 20). In fact, Bede says Ireland was already inhabited by "Scotti" when the "Scythian" Picts attempted to land there; thus Ireland "is properly the native land of the Irish; they emigrated from it [into Scotland] as we have described and so formed the third nation in Britain in addition to the Britons and the Scots" (21). In postconquest versions, the island is described as "wust & wylde" (Mannyng, *Story of England* I.128)—uninhabited—thus implying that the British king had the right to dispose of it at his will. In other words, this story could have been used to support the English claim on Ireland, as in fact it was.[16]

The source for this story in Middle English chronicles is Geoffrey of Monmouth's *Historia Regum Britanniae* (ca. 1136), which evidently draws some material from both Gildas and Nennius, especially regarding British/Irish relations. By 1155 the *Historia* had been translated into Anglo-Norman, and eventually had an enormous impact on English literature. Geoffrey became a prime source for most later chroniclers, especially in his portrayal of King Arthur as the great British hero who "was to outdo all other historical (and less historical) heroes."[17] Geoffrey's chronicle may have influenced the course of English history itself, particularly with regard to Ireland, according to Walter Ullmann, who points out that Giraldus Cambrensis, historian of the Norman conquest of Ireland in 1171 (*Expugnatio Hibernica,* 1189), "explicitly referred to Geoffrey's *Historia,* whose statements on the subjugation of Ireland by Gurguntius and later by Arthur furnished two of the five reasons why Ireland should be subjected to England."[18]

The passage Ullmann refers to is in the third part of the *Topographia,* and follows Geoffrey's account closely, except for Giraldus's statement that Ireland "was then either entirely uninhabited *or had been settled by [Gurguintius]*" (*History* 99, italics mine), a detail not found in any other chronicles, but which adds still more weight to Giraldus's argument that England was justified in claiming control of Ireland. Geoffrey identifies the exiles as "Basclenses," and Giraldus finds in this detail further support for his argument.

> [T]he city of Bayonne is on the boundary of Gascony, and belongs to it. It is also the capital of Basclonia, whence the Hibernienses came. And now Gascony and all Aquitaine rejoices in the same rule as Britain. (100)

Thus, according to Ullmann, the grant of Ireland to Henry II by the English Pope Adrian "'according to the right of inheritance,'" must have been based ultimately upon Geoffrey's "fictional history."[19]

In the fourteenth and fifteenth centuries, Giraldus's "historical" justification of English sovereignty over Ireland was further spread through the very popular *Polychronicon* of Ranulph Higden, who drew his chapters on Ireland largely from the *Topographia;* John Trevisa's Middle English translation also received wide circulation, and ends the story as follows: "þe kyng sent [the Basclenses] to Irlond þat was þoo voyde and wast, and ordeyned and sent wiþ hem dukes and lederes of his owne. And so hit semeþ þat Irlond schulde longe to Britayne by lawe of old tyme" (I.345).

Another "historical" even that the English would have found useful in justifying their claim to Ireland was the early conquest of

Ireland by King Arthur, a major episode in most of the postconquest chronicles. It first appears in Geoffrey of Monmouth (though Nennius was the first to mention Arthur by name), and again, Geoffrey is probably the source for later Middle English writers. The story begins with Uther Pendragon's expedition to Ireland, on Merlin's advice, to capture the "Giants' Ring" (i.e., Stonehenge),[20] intending to rebuild it on Salisbury Plain as a battle monument. The Irish, under "Gillomanius," attack the British, but are defeated. Gillomanius allies himself with the Saxon Paschent, who wants revenge on Uther for the death of Paschent's father Vortigern, and their armies invade Britain. They arrange for the poisoning of Uther's brother Aurelius. Enraged, Uther attacks and defeats the Irish and Saxons, killing both Gillomanius and Paschent (196–202).

After Arthur succeeds his father, the Irish again attack Britain, led by Gilmaurius (in later versions, the two Irish kings are usually conflated under this name). Arthur "cut them to pieces mercilessly and forced them to return home. Once he had conquered the Irish, he was at liberty once more to wipe out the Scots and Picts" (219). After he has united the whole of Britain, Arthur sets out to conquer Ireland.

> As soon as the next summer came round, Arthur fitted out a fleet and sailed off to the island of Ireland, which he was determined to subject to his own authority. The moment he landed, King Gilmaurius, about whom I have told you before, came to meet him with a numberless horde of his people ready to fight against him. However, when Arthur began the battle, Gilmaurius' army, which was naked and unarmed, was miserably cut to pieces where it stood, and ran away to any place where it could find refuge. Gilmaurius himself was captured immediately and forced to submit. The remaining princes of the country, thunderstruck by what had happened, followed their King's example and surrendered. The whole of Ireland was thus conquered. (221–22)

In spite of this victory, Arthur's troubles with Ireland are not over. Mordred rebels against the king, and brings "the Scots, Picts and Irish into his alliance, with anyone else whom he knew to be filled with hatred for his uncle" (258). In the final battle, "[on] Mordred's side there fell Chelric, Eglaf, Egbrict and Bruning, all of them Saxons; the Irishmen Gillapatric, Gillasel and Gillarvus; and the Scots and Picts, with nearly everyone in command of them" (261). This association of the Irish with other enemies of England is a recurring motif in the Middle English chronicles. The sense here is that the Irish, while they may have submitted under duress, continue to hold a grudge against their conquerors and may turn on them at any time—just as they were described by Giraldus.

> When you have employed every safeguard and used every precaution for your own safety and security, both by means of oaths and hostages, and friendships firmly cemented, and all kinds of benefits conferred, then you must be especially on your guard, because then especially their malice seeks a chance. . . .
> You must be more afraid of their wile than their war; their friendship than their fire; their honey than their hemlock; their shrewdness than their soldiery; their betrayals than their battle lines; their specious friendship than their enmity despised. . . . These are their characteristics: they are neither strong in war, nor reliable in peace. (*History* 106–7)

Similar accounts appear, sometimes in elaborate detail, in several of the Middle English chronicles. In fact, these Arthurian episodes include most of the references to Ireland in both Latin and vernacular English chronicles, except in the works of Giraldus Cambrensis. Laȝamon's version is over six thousand lines altogether (with one Irish king, "Gillomar"); Robert of Gloucester's about six hundred (Irish kings "Gyneman" and "Gillam"); seventeen pages in the prose *Brut* ("Guillomer"); and fifty-nine lines in Robert Manning of Brunne's *Story of England* ("Gwylomar"). King Arthur had captured the British imagination and his legend would continue to be elaborated upon in history and romance. Parallels were drawn between him and later kings, such as Edward III *(Prose Brut),* and the Tudors attempted to support their claim to the throne by tracing their line back to Arthur. Thus, starting with Geoffrey's account, Arthur's conquest of Ireland became a small but vital element in support of England's claim on the neighboring island.[21]

Ireland and the Irish in Laȝamon's *Brut*

Laȝamon, while drawing on Geoffrey for his account of Stonehenge and Arthur's conquest, includes additional detail concerning the Irish. Arguably, these specific details in the *Brut,* particularly those having to do with the clothing and weaponry of the Irish, indicate that Laȝamon may have been better acquainted with Ireland than any other chronicler after Giraldus Cambrensis.[22] Citing Laȝamon's "irrelevant" description of the ragged clothes worn by the first settlers of Ireland after their long sea voyage, followed

ɔy the statement that they continued this custom for a long time
(Laȝamon, I.3126–29), Tatlock points out that here

> the tatters and rags which travelers in Ireland have commented on for
> many a day are given a highly respectable history; the Irish are ragged
> because their forefathers' clothes wore out. . . . It is a fair conjecture
> that Lawman did not invent this, but is retailing a current excuse.[23]

Though Geoffrey had earlier stated that the Irish fought "naked
and unarmed" (221–22),[24] Laȝamon's descriptions of the Irish warriors undressing to go into battle naked (II.8658, 9011, 11147–48)
are remarkably vivid and he describes in detail the weapons they
use:

> þer isah Gillomar . whar him com Vther.
> 7 hæhde his cnihtes . to wepne forð-rihtes.
> 7 heo to biliue . 7 gripen heore cniues.
> 7 of mid here breches . seolcuðe weoren heore leches.
> 7 igripen an heore hond heore . speren longe.
> hengen an heore æxle . mucle wi-æxe.
>
> (II.8993–98)

> þa Irisce men weoren . nakede neh þan.
> mid spere 7 mid axen . 7 mide swiðe scærpe sæxen.
>
> (II.11147–48)

Other accounts verify these descriptions, including that of Giraldus, "Lawman's contemporary."[25] In fact, it seems equally possible
that Giraldus was Laȝamon's source.

> [T]hey go naked and unarmed into battle. . . . They use, however, three
> types of weapons—short spears, two darts (in this they imitate the
> Basclenses), and big axes well and carefully forged, which they have
> taken over from the Norwegians and the Ostmen. . . .
> From an old and evil custom they always carry an axe in their hand
> as if it were a staff. (*History* 101, 107)

However, Laȝamon is the only chronicler to record that the
Irish King Gillomar swears by St. Brendan (II.8642) and that after
Arthur has defeated the Irish and captured Gillomar, Gillomar
swears fealty to him, offering numerous tributes, including "sume
sixti" children to be fostered by Arthur, including his own son
(II.11,168–69), and relics of major Irish saints:

> ich wulle nimen . halidom.
> of seint Columkille . þe dude Godes iwille.
> 7 seint Brændenes hæfed . þe Godd seolf haleʒede.
> 7 seint Bride riht fot . þe hali is 7 swiðe god.
> 7 halidomes inoʒe . þe come ut of Rome.
>
> (II.11,178–81

These references to Irish saints also support the theory that Laʒamon may have been familiar with Ireland.[26] The reference to St. Columkille seems particularly significant, since St. Columkille rarely appears in English hagiography and "his name is in the form which has always been usual in Ireland . . . and elsewhere scarce and mostly due to Irish influence";[27] St. Patrick is more commonly found—"the first saint who would come to mind of an informed man who did not know Ireland well."[28] A detail I find even more convincing is the offer of children to be fostered at Arthur's court. Fosterage, the practice of a client sending his children to be raised in the household of his king, is referred to often in Irish sagas and law tracts; it seems to have less threatening implications than the simple exchange of hostages.

Where might Laʒamon have acquired this kind of specific information about Irish culture? Since we have no explicit evidence that he ever visited Ireland, one can only speculate. The prologue to *Brut* states that Laʒamon had "journeyed 'widely throughout the land' to gather sources for his work, though how 'widely' is open to question," according to the translator Donald G. Bzdyl.[29] J. S. P. Tatlock's analysis of Laʒamon's geographical references "suggest that [he] knew southern Wales and south and southwest England well."[30] In those areas, Laʒamon might well have encountered Irish clerics or merchants who could give him the sort of details reflected in the passages just cited.[31]

Whether or not Laʒamon had firsthand knowledge of Ireland and the Irish, his portrayal of them is nevertheless generally unfavorable. King Gillomar and the Irish are ridiculed for their overconfidence in attacking Arthur:

> 7 þe king Gillomar . gon him to fleonne þar,
> 7 flæh forð-rihtes . mid twenti of his cnihtes.
> in-to ænne muchele wude . wurðscipen biræiued.
> wes his Irisce uolc . mid stele iualled.
> þus wes þe king iscænd . 7 þus he endede his ʒelp.
> 7 þus to wude ferden . 7 lette his folc fællen.
>
> (II.8561–752)

ccording to Laȝamon, the Irish are allied with the Saxons and cots—enemies of England (II.8999–9042, 10884–93). After Gillomar submits to Arthur, the Irish become Arthur's allies, but the eputation for treachery they had acquired from Giraldus is reected in their inclusion among those Modred recruits for his rebelon against Arthur (II.14217–24). Laȝamon's accurate knowledge f Irish customs does not seem to have made him an admirer of he people.

Giraldus Cambrensis and Higden's *Polychronicon*

The one writer who goes into real detail concerning contemporary Ireland and Irish/British relations is Giraldus Cambrensis in is late twelfth-century Latin works, the *Topographia Hibernica* nd the *Expugnatio Hibernica*. Giraldus is the only medieval hronicler known to have visited Ireland and, though probably not n eyewitness himself of all the events he describes, was related o or acquainted with many of the Normans and Norman-Welsh vho had taken part in the original invasion.[32] He was a member f Prince John's unsuccessful expedition in 1185–86. On the one and, this makes his descriptions of Ireland and account of events here possibly the most accurate we have; on the other hand, he s extremely biased against the Irish and in favor of the Welsh-Normans (and, to a lesser extent, the Anglo-Normans). Perhaps the best excuse for Giraldus's negative descriptions of the Irish is given by A. B. Scott and F. X. Martin, the latest editors of the *Expugnatio Hibernica,* who maintain:

> There is no vindictiveness in his comments. He is simply stating the facts as he sees them . . . there was so much of Gaelic culture which Giraldus could not be aware of, simply because it was an orally transmitted rather than literate culture . . . [Giraldus] had no Irish, and therefore, presumably little or no contact with the Irish other than the small group of ecclesiastics who knew Latin. Irish society was technologically backward, and this backwardness in obvious things like housebuilding or weapon manufacture would also strike the outsider. Very often it seems as if Giraldus had got to hear just enough about Irish customs to misunderstand them and give a travestied account of them.[33]

Nevertheless, considering that, as Giraldus himself put it, "it is only when he who reports a thing is also one that witnessed it that anything is established on the sound basis of truth" (*History* 35),

medieval readers depended heavily upon Giraldus for information
concerning Ireland, and thus perpetuated at the same time many
outrageous slurs against the Irish.

There are at least seventeen manuscripts containing one or more
of Giraldus's works,[34] indicating that they were widely known. It
is difficult to say exactly how much Giraldus may have (directly
or indirectly) affected popular opinion concerning Ireland in the
thirteenth through fifteenth centuries, but presumably he had a
powerful influence. In addition to using Geoffrey of Monmouth's
version of the early settlement of Ireland to justify England's claim
there, Giraldus also emphasized that this claim had been confirmed
by the pope (*History* 100; *Expugnatio*). This confirmation is later
reflected in Capgrave's fifteenth-century *Abbreuiacion of Cronicles*.

> It was [Pope Adrianus II, an Englishman] þat graunted Kyng Herri þe
> Secunde to go into Yrlond and turne hem to þe feith, and to þat entent
> he made him lord of þe lond, on þis condicion, þat euery hous schuld
> paye ȝerli a Petir-peny to Rome. (108)

It was Ranulph Higden, however, who spread Giraldus's views
most liberally, as mentioned before. Higden's midfourteenth century *Polychronicon,* one of the most widely circulated works of
the time, was then translated twice into Middle English, by John
Trevisa (1385–87) and later by another, anonymous writer.[35] The
Polychronicon's account of Ireland opens with these words (all
quotations are from Trevisa's translation):

> Hibernia, þat is Irlond, and was of olde tyme incorporat in to þe
> lordschippe of Bretayne, so seiþ Giraldus in sua Topographia. Þere
> he descryueþ it at þe fulle, ȝit it is worþy and semelich to preise þat
> lond wiþ large preysinge. (I.329)

From the chapters that follow, it would seem that only the island
itself is praiseworthy. The people are characterized as generally
despicable. Regarding the land, Higden writes, citing Giraldus: "þe
holsomnesse [and helpe] of þat lond and þe clennesse wiþoute
venyme is worþ al þe boost and richesse of treen, of herbes, of
spicerie, of [riche] cloþes, and precious stones of þe est londes"
(I.333).[36] The description continues, detailing the many kinds of
game, fish, and agricultural products to be found in great abundance in Ireland, and also acknowledging that some types of animals and plants are not found there, including (of course) snakes
(I.329–39).

Regarding the Irish people, however, Higden quotes first Giraldus' fairly straightforward description of the people and their customs of dress, riding, weapons, and livelihood; he acknowledges their musical skill (I.353–55).[37] Interspersed throughout these passages are jabs such as "þey beeþ vnsemeliche of maneres and of cloþyng" (I.353)[38] and "Þey vse no craft of flex and wolle, of metal, noþer of marchaundise; but ȝeueþ hem alle to idelnesse and to sleuþe" (I.355).[39] But much more space is given to detailing the repulsive and barbarous qualities of the Irish (I.355–61, 377–81).[40] For example:

Þese men beeþ of yuel maneres and of leuynge; þey paieþ none teþinges, þei weddeþ lawefulliche non wyfes, þey spareþ not her alies, bot þe broþer weddeþ his broþer wyf. Þey beeþ besy forto betraye hire neiȝbores and oþere. . . . Among hem longe vsage and euel custume haþ so long i-dured, þat . . . as þei be traytoures by kynde, so aliens and men of straunge londes þat woneþ longe among hem draweþ aftir þe manere of hir companye, and skapeþ wel vnneþe but þey be i-smotted wiþ þe schrewednesse and bycomeþ traytours also. . . . Þere beeþ meny men in þis lond wonder foule and yuel i-schape yn lymes and in body. For in hir lymes lakkeþ þe benefice of kynde, so þat nowher beeþ no better i-schape, þan þey þat beeþ þere wel i-schape; and no-wher non worse i-schape þan þey þat beeþ þere euel i-schape. . . . Here Girald makeþ mencioun, þat as men of þis nacioun beeþ more angry þan oþer men and more hasty for to take wreche, while þey beeþ on lyue; so seyntes and halowes of þis lond beeþ more wrecheful þan seyntes of oþer londes." (I.355–59, 377)[41]

Higden omits some of the more bizarre details given by Giraldus—for example, the sensational account of how the king of a certain clan in Ulster is confirmed in office by copulating with a mare, which is then killed and cooked and the meat distributed to the people (*History* 109–10); or Giraldus' remarkably prejudiced tale of certain Irishmen from a remote region of Connacht who

had never before seen . . . the trappings of civilization. . . . Nor did they know anything about the year, nor the month, nor the week, and they were completely ignorant of the names of the days of the week . . . they had as yet heard nothing of Christ and knew nothing about him. (*History* 111)

However, Higden sometimes goes beyond Giraldus in describing the barbarous qualities of the Irish, either by citing other sources, or by distorting Giraldus. For example, Higden's chapter describing the Irish people begins with a reference to Solinus, his other main source of information about Ireland:

> Solinus seiþ þat men of þis lond beeþ straunge of nacioun, housles, and grete fiȝteres, and acounteþ riȝt and wrong al for oon, and beeþ sengle of cloþing, scarse of mete, cruel of herte and angry of speche, and drinkeþ firste blood of dede men þat beeþ i-slawe, and þan wassheþ her face þerwiþ; and holdeþ hem apayde wiþ flesshe and fruit instede of mete, and wiþ mylk instede of drynke, and vseþ moche playes and hydelnesse and huntynge, and trauailleþ ful litel. (I.351–53)

After reading that the Irish drink the blood of slain men and wash their faces with it, the next statement—that they eat simply, content with meat, fruit, and milk—carries little weight. In addition, the way Trevisa has translated Higden's sentence ("Carnibus et fructibus pro esu, lacte pro potu contenta" [I.352]) makes these harmless habits seem at least rather peculiar, if not actually wicked. Also, in the next sentence, hunting is presented not as a necessary pursuit of food but as a type of "playes and hydelnesse"—which it may well have been in more agriculturally oriented England.

In his treatment of Irish clergy, Higden's paraphrasing distorts Giraldus' account so that the Irish priests come off much worse. The passage just cited regarding the vindictiveness of Irish saints, is in fact directly translated from Giraldus. However, where Giraldus wrote:

> The clergy of this country are on the whole to be commended for their observance. Among their other virtues chastity shines out as a kind of special prerogative. They diligently carry out their obligations in the matter of the Psalms and the hours, reading and praying. They . . . fulfill the divine offices with which they are entrusted. They practice a considerable amount of abstinence and asceticism in the use of food. Most of them, in fact, fast daily all day long until twilight, when they have completed all the offices of the hours of the day.
>
> But it would be better if after their long fasts they were as sober as they are late in coming to food, as sincere as they are severe, as pure as they are dour, and as genuine as they appear. (*History* 112)

Higden's version omits Geraldus's more positive comments, and expands upon the subtle reproof of the last paragraph.

> Clerkes of þis lond beeþ chast, and biddeþ meny bedes, and dooþ greet abstinence a day, and drynkeþ al nyȝt; so þat it is accounted for a myracle þat leccherie reigneþ nouȝt þere, as wyn reigneþ. (I.377–79)

Giraldus goes on to complain that although the Irish clergy are diligent enough in their monastic observances, they neglect evangelism and the work of exhorting their sinful parishioners to repent (*History* 112–15). He points out that a peculiar shortcoming of the Irish church is that it has no martyrs, and recounts a conversation he had with an Irish bishop.

When once upon a time I was making these complaints . . . to Tatheus, the archbishop of Cashel, a learned and discreet man, . . . and was blaming the prelates especially for the terrible enormities of the country, using the very strong argument that no one had ever in that kingdom won the crown of martyrdom in defence of the church of God, the archbishop gave a reply which cleverly got home—although it did not rebut my point: "It is true," he said, "that although our people are very barbarous, uncivilized, and savage, nevertheless they have always paid great honour and reverence to churchmen, and they have never put out their hands against the saints of God. But now a people has come into the kingdom which knows how, and is accustomed, to make martyrs. From now on Ireland will have its martyrs, just as other countries." (*History* 115–16)

Higden's condensed version of this conversation again omits Giraldus's respectful characterization of Tatheus and adds some phrases that emphasize the negative.

What clerkes and prelates schulde doo is to hem vnknowe; þerfore whan it was i-putte aȝenst þe bisshop of Casille, how it myȝte be þat so meny seyntes beeþ in Irlond and neuere a martir among ham, *sippe þat þe men beeþ so schrewed and so angry,* and þe prelates so recheles and so slowh in correcciouns of trespas, þe bisshop answerde forwardliche i-now, and seide: "Oure men beþ schrewed and angry inow to hem self, but in Goddes servauntes þey leye neuere no hond, but þey dooþ hem greet reuerence and worschippe; but Englische men comeþ in to þis lond, þat konneþ make martires and were i-woned to vse þat craft." (I.379–81, italics mine)

It must also be noted, however, that Higden, writing in the fourteenth century, has no qualms about going on to explain the bishop's comment by saying, "Þe bisshop seide so, bycause þat kyng Henry þe secounde was þoo i-come in to Irlond freschliche after þe martirdom of Seint Thomas of Caunturbury" (I.381), a comment Giraldus, writing in the service of that same king, would never have dared make, though perhaps he had it in mind.

Later Middle English Chronicles—Ireland as Untamed Backwater

Most of the later chronicles are rather sketchy in their recording of events closer to their own times, even though the writers, especially in the fourteenth and fifteenth centuries, were more likely to have available to them more reliable contemporary sources, such as official documents and open letters that often served as news dispatches.[42] One possible reason for this brevity is that during this time England was preoccupied with political affairs at home and on the Continent, and gave scant attention to her Irish colonies;[43] in fact, I found no references to fifteenth-century events in Ireland, with the possible exception of "The Twelve Letters to Save Merry England," a political poem dated 1460–61 in praise of "the four principal Yorkist heroes,"[44] Edward, Earl of March (Edward IV); his father Richard, Duke of York; Richard, Earl of Warwick; and his father, Richard, Earl of Salisbury. The two relevant stanzas are as follows:

> An F. for þe feterlock þat is of grete substance,
> That hathe amendide many materes þorow his mediacion;
> In yrlonde and in wales, in englonde and in fraunce,
> He Reynyed with Rewelis of Riall Repetacion.

> An R. for the Rose that is frische and wol nat fade,
> Bothe þe rote and the stalke þat is of grete honore,
> from normandie unto norway þe leves do springe
> from irlonde unto Estlonde me reioise þat floure. (41–48)[45]

These and the other letters "comprise the initials of the names, titles and badges" of the four men (Scattergood 191).[46] In the first stanza, Ireland is simply part of the English realm; in the second stanza, it is the western limit of Edward's acclaim. However, Ireland was a noted center of support for the Yorkist cause.[47]

Another consideration is that if relatively recent events had taken place under the current dynasty or involved members of a noble patron's family, the chroniclers might be reluctant to risk expanding upon or interpreting them in greater detail, especially if an incident showed the patron or his family in an unflattering light.[48] For example, Robert of Gloucester notes that Richard the Marshall was killed at Kildare in Ireland "through treason of his owne men" (II.10/782–809). Other English chronicles indicated more explicitly that these men were Richard's Irish vassals,[49] but in fact Richard had been the victim of a plot condoned (if not initiated) by King Henry III and carried out by Richard de Burgh and others.[50]

In numerous references to Ireland and the Irish in the fourteenth century, Middle English chronicles reflect a view of Ireland as an untamed backwater inhabited by dangerous natives. Possibly the earliest known reference in Middle English to "wild Irishmen" is found in the *Prose Brut* (late fourteenth century), in a distressing account of the death of the Earl of March during the reign of Richard II.

> The which Erle . . . went ouyr see yn-to Irelond vnto his lordeschippez and londez, for the Erle of March is Erle of Vlcestre yn Irelonde . . . and þere come apon hym a grete multitude of buschmentis of wilde Iryschmen, hym for to take and distroye . . . and þere he was take, and hew al to pecis, and þere he deied; on whose soule God haue merci! Amen! (II.341/12–23)

The term "wild Irishmen" swiftly came into common usage[51] and became part of a "tradition that . . . continued unbroken well on into the English Romantic movement."[52] The "wild Irish" appear again as this chronicle goes on to record briefly the expedition of Richard II to Ireland in 1394, making it sound much simpler than it probably was.[53]

> Thanne King Richarde made gret ordynaunce, and went ouyr see Into Irelond. . . .
>   And þanne he passed þe see, and come ynto Irelonde, and þere he was welle and worthily resceyued. And þese rebellis of Ireland bith callid "wilde Irisch men"; and anon her chefteynez & hir gouernoures & leeders comyn down vnto þe King, & yolde ham vnto hym . . . & þus he conqueryd þe moste party of Irelond in a litil tyme (II.356–57)

A satirical poem of the same period, *Richard the Redeles,* also refers to this successful expedition: "Of Richard þat Regned so Riche and so noble, / That whyle he werred be west on þe wilde yrisshe. . . ."[54]

Restless natives were not the only problems encountered by the English colonists. In the later chronicles, it seems clear that Ireland was the kind of place few Englishmen would visit or live in voluntarily. The idea of Ireland as a place of exile goes back at least to Bede (195 passim), where exile is a form of religious discipline.[55] But the *Prose Brut* (late fourteenth century) records how Parliament forced Edward II to send his favorite, Piers Gaveston, into exile in Ireland (I.206/20–22; cf. Capgrave's *Abbreuaicion of Cronicles* 136–37). Similarly, among the entries having to do with Ireland and the Irish in Capgrave's *Abbreuiacion of Cronicles* (completed ca. 1462–63) is an account of the conflict concerning the appointment of the duke of Gloucester as duke of Ireland [1392]. "And anon as he was absent his enmyes in þe kyngis hous cried on þe kyng to clepe him ageyn. It was perel, as þei seide, þat he schuld go for making of rebelles in þat wilde lond" (201). Here again (by implication) are the "wild Irish" and Ireland itself as a wild, unpredictable region.

Gloucester was replacing the disgraced Robert de Vere, who, it is interesting to note, seems never to have set foot in Ireland. De Vere's case is among those detailed by John Lydgate in *The Sudden Fall of Princes* (ca. 1431–38):

> Þis duc of Yrland, of England chaumburleyn
> Which in plesaunce so he ledde his lyff,
> Tyl fortune of his welthe had disdeyn,
> Þat causeles he parted was from his wyff,
> Which grounde was of gret debate and stryff,
> And his destruccion, if I shal not lye,
> For banned he was, and did in meschef dye.[56]

De Vere was the ninth earl of Oxford (1362–92) and hereditary Great Chamberlain of England. According to Robinson's note,

> he was nominated Governor of Ireland in 1385, and created Duke of Ireland in 1386, although he did not leave England. Discontent against him rising, he was accused by the King's uncle, Thomas of Woodstock . . . , and defeated in battle in 1387. He escaped to Holland, where he learned of his sentence of death passed in 1388; he stayed in France until 1389, and then fled to Louvain. He was killed by a boar while hunting, in 1392. . . .[57]

An account of de Vere's divorce, which led to his disgrace, appears in Capgrave's *Abbreuiacion of Cronicles* (1462–63).

> In þis ȝere Robert Ver, whom þe kyng had mad duke of Erland, ros in so grete pride of hert þat, ageyn þe lawe of God, he refused his wif, a fayre woman and good, and eke born of grete blood, for Kyng Edward

dowtir was hir modyr. The woman whech he weddid aftir þis rejeccion cam oute of Bem, a sadeler doutir, hir name was Lancecrone. The kyng gaf fauour to þis mater, but þe lordes were wroth with it, specialy þe duke of Gloucestir, vncle of the forseid Ysabel,[58] þat þoute sumtyme to set remedy in þis mater. (191–92)

Dukes of Ireland who had either never visited the territory, such as de Vere, or who could not be trusted to live there, such as Gloucester, are just two examples of a continuing probem in England: Anglo-Irish landowners and Gaelic Irish (either submissive or rebellious) residing in England. In another entry of 1392, Capgrave records that so many of the Irish had made their way to England that the English seem to have felt threatened both at home and abroad.

In þe mont of Auguste [1392] it was proclamed þorowoute Ynglond þat all Erischmen be at hom in her owne lond in þe fest of natiuité of oure Lady, in peyne of lesyng of her hed. For it was proued by experiens that þere were com to Ynglond so many Erishmen þat þe Erich cuntré, whech longeth to þe king of Ynglond, was so voyded fro his dwelleris þat þe wilde Erisch were com in and had dominacioun of al þat cuntré. (203)

That these people in England are referred to as simply "Erischmen," rather than "Erisch lords" (as elsewhere in this chronicle) implies that they were not necessarily the aristocratic Hiberno-English, but included Gaelic Irish loyal to England living in areas under English control.[59] The English government attempted to deal with the situation by passing a series of "absentee acts from 1368 onwards."[60] The absentee acts were directed primarily at Anglo-Irish colonists who had abandoned their lands, but in practice the acts were also applied to any "undesirable" Gaelic Irish, who might be accused of being "Irish rebels" or "wild Irish," although many of them, such as university students and clergymen, were in England for perfectly legitimate purposes.[61] Martin points out that the "complaints" against the Irish residents "were not balanced with the fact that one of the most influential chancellors of the University of Oxford (1332–34) was Richard FitzRalph from Dundalk, later archbishop of Armagh (1344–60)."[62] In matters of politics, however, the people's memory has ever been short.

Capgrave's chronicle (which draws on a wide variety of sources) emphasizes the role that these and other Irish troubles played in the eventual downfall of Richard II, noting especially the financial burdens laid on England by Richard's efforts to control rebellion in Ireland.

> [I]t was noted þat in Kyng Edward tyme þe þirde, whan he had set þere his bank, his juges, and his chekyr, he receyued euery ȝere xxx m pound, and now þe Kyng Richard was fayn to paye ȝerly, to defens of þe same cuntré [i.e., Ireland], xxx m mark. . . . (203)

Although in the following year the Duke of Gloucester was able to present Parliament with a convincing case for supporting the king in Ireland, so that "þe clergy graunted him a dyme and þe lay-fe a fiftene" (203), the financing of Richard's 1399 expedition, undertaken to avenge the death of Roger Mortimer, Earl of March, was disastrous. Richard "purueyed mech þing of his ligis, and payed rite not, so þat ny all men hated him. . . ." (210) and while he was away, Henry of Lancaster (Henry IV) took advantage of this situation to mount a successful rebellion in England, ultimately forcing Richard to hand the crown over to him (210–14). A contemporary satirical poem, *Mum and the Sothsegger* (late fourteenth century, about the same time as the *Prose Brut*) capsulizes this expedition[63] and also mentions "the wild Irish":

> So sore were þe sawis / of bothe two sidis,
> Of Richard þat regned / so riche and so noble,
> That wyle he werrid be west / on þe wilde Yrisshe,
> Henrri was entrid / on þe est half,
> Whom all þe londe loued / in lengþe and in brede. . . .[64]

Some Positive Exceptions

Did medieval English chroniclers have anything good to say about Ireland and the Irish? Very little. In fact, it sometimes seems as if Middle English writers deliberately ignored the few positive statements found in their sources. For example, some for whom Bede is a source of other information do not use his numerous mentions of Irish clerics who exhibited extraordinary piety, scholarship, and evangelistic zeal. This may be only because it was not relevant to their secularly oriented works. One exception is Higden, who includes accounts of St. Patrick, of the misison of St. Columba and St. Gall to Germany, and of the Vision of Fursa (V.231, 303–7, 387–89, 461; VI.7–15). Giraldus, also, admits that "the clergy of this country are on the whole to be commended for their observance" (*History* 112), though Higden's paraphrase of this passage, as translated by Trevisa, overwhelms that brief commendation with denigrating information, as just discussed.

Giraldus himself has a few positive comments, as Scott and Martin point out in their introduction to the *Expugnatio.*

> Like some nineteenth-century British imperialists he is willing to acknowledge that there are "good" natives. Thus he blames John and his entourage for alienating Irishmen who had remained loyal to the Normans since the coming of FitzStephen. He describes Domnall of Limerick as *vir sua in gente non improvidus* [a man not without forethought among his own people]—though perhaps this is a rather backhanded compliment.[65]

In the *Topographia,* Giraldus gives a detailed and very enthusiastic description of Irish music, saying, "It is only in the case of musical instruments that I find any commendable diligence in the people. They seem to me to be incomparably more skilled in these than any other people that I have seen" (*History* 103). Higden quotes this passage fairly completely (I.355).

In "The Siege of Calais" (1436) at least one Irishman makes a good showing against the French and Flemish, who had besieged the English in Calais in July 1435:[66]

> There myght men see Archers gode
> Cast away both gowne and hode
>   The better forto shote;
> The frenshe and flemmyssh were ful fayn
> To thaire tentes retourne ageyn,
>   þey saw noon other bote.
>
> And euer among an Irissh man
> On his hoby that swiftly ran;
>   It was a sportful sight
> How his dartes he did shake;
> And whan hym lust to leue or take,
>   They had full grete dispite.
>
> (115–26)[67]

The description is rather comical: the Irishman "on his hoby" (122), a small pony, compared to the war horses of the English, and the lines "It was a sportful sight / How his dartes he did shake" (123–24), which refer to the preferred weapons of the native Irish: short-throwing spears. Nevertheless, the Irishman and his darts do quite a bit of damage. "They had full grete dispite" (126).

Higden, and to some extent Caxton's *Mirrour of the World,* include glowing descriptions of Irish geography, flora, and fauna (*Polychronicon* I.329–39); a good deal of this information came from Giraldus. For example: "In þis lond is plente of hony and of mylk and of wyn, and noȝt of vyneȝerdes" (*Polychronicon* I.337).[68] Giraldus, and thence Higden/Trevisa also acknowledged certain failings in the country as well.

> Whete cornes beeþ þere ful smal, vnneþe i-clansed wiþ manis hond; out take men, alle bestes beeþ smallere þere þan in oþer londes. Þere lackeþ wel nyh al manere of fresche water fische, þat is nouȝt gendred in þe see; þere lakkeþ vnkynde faukouns, girefaukouns, partriche, fesauntes, nyȝtingales, and pies. Þere lakkeþ also roo and bukke. . . . (*Polychronicon* I.337–39; cf. *History* 34, 37–38, 47–48)

It should be noted, however, that not all "lacks" are negative; Ireland also "lakkeþ . . . venemous bestes," thanks to St. Patrick.

> For venemous bestes and wormes deyeþ þere anon, and me brynge hem þider out of oþer londes; and also venym and poysoun, i-brouȝt þiderward out of oþer londes, leseþ his malys anon as he passeþ þe myddel of þe see. (*Polychronicon* I.339; cf. *History* 50–52)

Laȝamon, in recounting Arthur's exploits following his conquest of Ireland, often includes Ireland in lists of nations who support Arthur. After helping Arthur rout the Saxons, the Irish are invited to the victory feast (II.11346–59); preparing to invade France, he receives warriors from his subject kingdoms, including "elleuen þusend" from Ireland (II.11655–63); the Irish King Gillomar is among his retinue as they attack Paris (II.11877–901); at a big festival at "Kairliun" on Whitsunday, the long list of eminent personages attending includes Gillomar (II.12166); Arthur invades Italy, with Irishmen in his army (II.12686). Tatlock says that Laȝamon shows "both kindness toward Ireland and knowledge of it,"[69] but it seems more significant that in all of Laȝamon's most favorable references, Ireland appears as England's vassal.

To sum up, the picture of Ireland that emerges from medieval English chronicles, both in Latin and Middle English, is at best incomplete, and at worst highly distorted in such a way as to favor English political claims there. Originally such distortions may not have been deliberate, but they were perpetuated by uncritical use of source materials. Distorted views of Ireland are manifested in two ways. First, through accounts of prehistoric and pseudohistoric encounters between England and Ireland which suggest that

England has a legitimate claim on Ireland—the story of King Arthur's victory over the Irish King Gillomar is the primary example. Second, through various portrayals of the Irish people themselves as "wild" and "barbarous," treacherous, cruel, and (occasionally) heretical—in other words, a race that either deserves to be conquered as a form of retribution, or else that needs to be conquered in order to be "disciplined and civilized."[70] Giraldus Cambrensis is the most adamant proponent of this approach, but it also appears in accounts of Richard II's late fourteenth-century Irish expeditions and in the Arthur legends. Colonial Ireland became a convenient place of exile for nobles in political disfavor, which further emphasized its image as an uncivilized, faraway hardship post.

3

Ireland and the Irish in Middle English Romances

Ireland appears in a number of Middle English romances, mostly Arthurian. These include, in roughly chronological order: the Arthurian sections of Laʒamon's *Brut* (ca. 1220), *Of Arthoure and of Merlin* (1250–1300), *Sir Tristrem* (late thirteenth century), *Lybeaus Desconus* (ca. 1325), the alliterative *Morte Arthure* (ca. 1400), *Sir Launfal* (late fourteenth century), the stanzaic *Morte Arthure* (ca. 1400), Henry Lovelich's *History of the Holy Grail* (ca. 1425) and *Merlin* (1400–1450), the *Prose Merlin (ca. 1450),* and Malory's *Le Morte Darthur* (ca. 1470).[1] These all deal with Arthur's conquest of Ireland, and ultimately derive from Geoffrey of Monmouth. Other, miscellaneous romances include *King Horn* (ca. 1225), *Guy of Warwick* (ca. 1300), *Horn Childe* (ca. 1320), and the *Romauns of Partenay* (ca. 1500).[2]

In some of these romances Ireland seems to serve as merely another strange foreign land where the hero has adventures. The actual location of such countries seems irrelevant when, as in the *Alliterative Morte Arthure,* Ireland is included with lands such as Africa and Austria that are improbably distant from the English scene of battle, in order to magnify Arthur's conquest:

> The kynge comly over-keste knyghtes and othire,
> Erlles of Awfrike, and Estriche berynes
> Of Orgaile and Orekenay, the Iresche kynges,
> The nobileste of Norwaye, nowmbirs fulle hugge,
> Dukes of Danamarkes, and dubbid knyghtes. . . .
>
> (ll. 3932–36)

"Iresche kynges" here also serve an alliterative purpose—in any case, the location or reality of Ireland is no more relevant than that of "Awfrike."

Similarly, in *Lybeaus Desconus* the hero, on his way from London to the Midlands, travels "Among aventurus fyle / Jn Yrland

and yn Wales" (1223–24), which, as the editor points out, would mean going quite a bit out of his way if we took it literally.[3] And in Lovelich's *History of the Holy Grail,* Joseph of Arimathea travels

> Al Abowte
> Into straunge Contres, with-Owten douwte,
> Into Scotland, Wales, & Into yrland,
> and Into manye Oþer partyes, I vndirstand
>
> (chap. 52, ll. 25–28)

In contexts such as these, we may assume that Ireland has much the same significance as "Ermonie" (Armenia), Sir Tristrem's supposed native land: "the Ermonie of *Sir Tristrem* belongs to the same unmapped country as the maritime Bohemia of Shakespeare."[4] Perhaps it is significant, however, that in both examples, the named "straunge Contres" are the Celtic borders of England.[5]

Ireland as Otherworld Island

But in many romances, Ireland is clearly meant to be that island to the west of England. It is the last known land before the uncharted open sea, yet not very well-known by the English, who perhaps were quite ready to believe that Ireland was the original site of Stonehenge, once known as "the giants' ring," and that a gateway into Hell (St. Patrick's Purgatory) could still be found there. Ranulph Higden, describing Ireland in his *Polychronicon* (1352; trans. John Trevisa 1387), noted that

> in þe vttermeste endes of þe world falleþ ofte newe meruailles and wondres, as þei kynde pleyde wiþ larger leue priueliche and fer in þe endes þan openliche and nyȝ in þe myddel. Þerfore in þis ilond beeþ meny grisliche meruayles and wondres. (I.361)

Giraldus included in his late twelfth-century *Historia et Topographia Hibernica,* a long list of bizarre and magical features of the island and its inhabitants, many of which were then incorporated into Higden's *Polychronicon,* the most widely circulated chronicle of the Middle English period.[6]

> Meny men telleþ þat in þe norþ side of Irlond is þe ilond of lyf; in þat ilond is no man þat may deie. . . . In Vltonia is an ilond in a lake departed wonderliche atweyne; in þe oon partie is ofte grete destourbaunce and discomfort of fendes, and in þe oþer partie greet likynge

and coumfort of aungelles. . . . In Mamonia is a welle; who þat
wascheþ hym wiþe þe water of þat welle . . . he schal worþe hoor.
Þere is anoþer welle in Vltonia, who þat is i-wasche þerynne, he schal
neuere wexe hoor afterward. (trans. Trevisa, I.361–65)

Higden adds further wonders, such as women who transform themselves into rabbits, magical swine made out of straw or grass which
revert to their own shape if they cross water (I.361), and a lake
that turns wood into iron and stone (I.369). Thus, while Ireland
remains in this world's geography, its characteristics are more
those of an island in the Otherworld.

The Otherworld is one of the major motifs in medieval literature,[7]
and most frequently manifests itself as either underground or as
an island.[8] The Otherworld need not be the land of the dead. It
may be an earthly paradise, or simply a different world—much like
our own, yet governed by different rules of time, space, and causal-
ity, so that magic, not logic, is the rule. According to T. McAlindon,
"It presents a world . . . whose outstanding phenomena, be they
only projections of things familiar, yet differ from them in the su-
perlative degree or are presented in such novel compounds as to
constitute new kinds."[9]

The earliest appearances of this Otherworld island or series of
islands are in classical works such as the *Aeneid,* or the works of
Poseidonius. Otherworld islands are also found in early Irish texts
such as the *Voyages* of Bran and of Maelduin. The island is usually
to be found in the west, and whether it is one island or a series (as
in the *Voyages*), its Otherworldly nature is revealed by the marvelous sights and adventures found there. In Middle English literature,
especially in the romances, Ireland itself often serves as an Otherworld island.

To begin with, a water barrier "is a feature in some form or
other common to almost all the accounts" of the Otherworld.[10]
Sometimes it is merely a river, such as the Styx, but often it is the
open sea—again, Ireland fits very well. H. R. Patch called the
Otherworld island motif "all but universal,"[11] but in searching for
possible sources for Middle English versions of an "Otherworldly"
Ireland, we know that many Latin manuscripts of the *Voyage of
St. Brendan* were extant all over Europe, and that it was translated
into Anglo-Norman in the early twelfth century in England. In the
Voyage of St. Brendan, Ireland, though not Otherwordly itself, is
the jumping-off place for the saint's journey into the unknown. He
discovers one marvelous island after another, some with theologi-
cal meanings—such as the island of fallen angels—some simply

amazing, such as the island of laughter or the island of gigantic sheep. Perhaps the earliest description of an Otherworldly Ireland is given by the Welsh chronicler Nennius in the *Historia Britonum,* recounting how the three sons of Mil Espagne came to Ireland and found there "a glassy tower in the midst of the sea" inhabited by people who would not reply when spoken to. When the soldiers and their followers landed on the island, the sea "overwhelmed them and they were drowned" (20). The silence of the inhabitants (typical of the dead[12]) and the disastrous consequences of landing on the island, strongly suggest the Otherworld.

Another element of the Otherworld as island is described by H. R. Patch in "The Adaptation of Otherworld Motifs to Medieval Romance":

> the journey by boat in helpless fashion to a realm where there is a princess who becomes the hero's amie. . . . [O]ne may see here a dovetailing of that idea with another, that of the rudderless boat that takes the hero to the Otherworld, where the fée awaits him.[13]

The motif of the voyage in a rudderless boat is found in the Irish voyage tales, for example, St. Brendan's curragh, in which he sets forth without any idea of where he is going. The fairy "amie" is an element of Irish *echtrai,* tales of adventures in the Otherworld.[14] Sir Tristram, having been put to sea to die after receiving a poisoned wound from an Irish knight, "travels in a rudderless boat at least before landing [in Ireland], and . . . we also have the meeting with the heroine who heals him and at this point is clearly of the fairy mistress type":[15]

> A wind to wil him bare
> To a stede þer him was boun
> Neiʒe hand:
> Deluelin hiʒt þe toun
> An hauen in irland.

(ll. 1162–66)

The hero of *King Horn* also crosses the sea to Ireland, fleeing from enemies in his homeland of Westernesse, and though his ship can be steered, his arrival in Ireland seems more a result of the chance direction of the wind than of Horn's intention:

> To hauene he [him] ferde
> A god schup he [him] h[er]de
> Þat him scholde l[e]de

[Vt of Westernesse þede];
[Þe whyȝt him gan wel stonde]
[And drof to Irelonde]

(ll. 769–74)

The concept of Ireland as Otherworld already existed in British literature, before the Norman Conquest. Proinsias Mac Cana describes how, in early Welsh literature, the Otherworld and Ireland become interchanged in three parallel accounts of expeditions to obtain a magic cauldron.

[*Preiddeu Annwn*] purports to give some account of a raid on the Otherworld carried out by Arthur and three shiploads of men. . . . The object of the expedition was to seize the cauldron of the Chief of Annwn. . . . In *Culhwch ac Olwen* there is a variant of this adventure . . . in which the Otherworld island has become Ireland. . . .

In *Branwen* we have what might be regarded as a third version of this overseas or Otherworld raid. It has an expedition to Ireland, an Irish—or Otherworld—cauldron as a central element, and a battle from which only seven of the Britons escaped. . . .

Whatever its precise form and content, some version of the Other World expedition was known to the author of *Branwen*. He had it in mind when he wrote his account of Bendigeidfran's journey to Ireland. . . .[16]

This is not to imply that the Middle English romancers or their audience were necessarily familiar with the Welsh material. It seems reasonable, however, that, as Patch puts it:

Much of this wealth of description [of the Otherworld] was not confined to what was written—that is to say, to the documents that have survived—but was floating in the medieval air of faith and credulity and artistic interest, and was transmitted by the channels of folktale and even popular rumor based on avid memory and long, long thoughts. Thus oriental culture, the religious life of Greece and Rome, the Jewish tradition, and Celtic and the Norse, could furnish details of the Other World [*sic*] even for writers who could hardly recognize their own indebtedness.[17]

Ireland in Middle English romances is a land of marvels, magical lore, and monsters. For example, according to Laȝamon's *Brut* and the *Prose Merlin,* Stonehenge was originally located in Ireland until Merlin directed its transfer to Salisbury Plain as a monument to Uther's victory there. "[H]it hatte þere Eotinde Ring," says Merlin (Laȝamon II.8622), and the remarkable thing about the stones, other than their size, is that water which runs off them is used for healing baths, as Merlin explains:

> þa stanes beo[ð] muchele . 7 mahten heo habbeoð.
> þa men þe beoð un-hal . heo fareð to þan stane.
> 7 heo wasced þene stan . 7 þer-mide baðied heore ban.
> umbe lutle stu[n]de . heo wurðed al isunde.
> (Laȝamon II.8577–80)

Other instances of magical remedies to be found in Ireland are found in Malory, whose Tristram must go to Ireland after he is wounded by the Irish Sir Marhalt's poisoned spear, since the wound can only be healed in the land from which the poison came.[18] And in the northern English *Sir Tristrem*, the Irish queen, mother of Ysonde, prepares a love potion intended for Ysonde and King Mark, which is mistakenly consumed by Ysonde and Tristram (ll. 1644–50).

Sir Tristrem's Ysonde may be an example of the fairy mistress who is one typical inhabitant of the Otherworld,[19] but the fairy mistress may be good or evil. Thomas Chestre's *Sir Launfal* (late fourteenth century) contains a unique example of the wicked type in "Gwennere," King Arthur's queen, who, though not specifically stated to be a fairy, is identified as the daughter of King Ryon of Ireland. This is unusual, for Guinevere is commonly described as coming of British or French stock, and presented as virtuous, with the lamentable exception of her adultery with either Lancelot or Mordred. Of this Irish Gwennere, however, Chestre writes:

> Sir Launfal lykede her noȝt,
> Ne oþer knyȝtes þat were hende;
> For þe lady bar los of swych word
> Þat sche hadde lemmanys unþer here lord,
> So fele þere nas noon ende.
> (ll. 44–48)

She also fails to bestow gifts on Sir Launfal, evidently because she knows he disapproves of her, which doesn't improve matters between them:

> Þe Quene yaf [g]yftes for þe nones
> Gold and seluere and precyous stonys,
> Here curtasye to kyþe;

> Euerych knyȝt sche ȝaf broche oþer ryng,
> But Syr Launfal sche yaf no þyng—
> Þat greuede hym many a syde.

(ll. 67–72)

Hoping to be rid of this thorny knight, the Irish Queen Gwennere eventually sends Sir Launful on the central quest of the romance, clearly hoping he will never return.

Another possible example of the fairy mistress is the speaker of the little verse, "Ich am of irlaunde," found among the collection in Manuscript Rawlinson D 913:

> Ich am of irlaunde,
> ant of the holy londe
> of irlande.
>
> Gode sire, pray ich the,
> for of saynte charite,
> come ant daunce wyt me
> in irlaunde.[20]

It is not, of course, a romance, but "appears to be either genuine folk-song or something closely modelled upon genuine folk-song, as is the case with the other bits of verse on the same leaf."[21] John Speirs suggests that the poem is part of a ritual dance or game, one of "the sacred dances of the ancient Nature religion which were still being kept up (whether or not the reasons for doing so were consciously realized) as the May and Midsummer ritual of the medieval folk."[22] In this highly speculative context, Speirs suggests that

> Ireland, the Isle of Saints because earlier it had been the Isle of the Gods, is here sacred still perhaps in a pagan as well as a Christian sense. The dancer from across the sea—from a sacred or magical *other* country—is still perhaps essentially a faery or otherworld visitant (or a human impersonator of such a character in the performed dance). Essentially, or symbolically, the dancer will steal away or abduct her partner. . . . The dancer thus becomes, almost in a literal sense, *enchanted* and *enchanting*. This particular song, chiefly by means of its rhythm and repetitions of sound, suggests to the reader a trance-like or rapt condition in the dancer whose song it is; consequently, a supernaturally compelling or appealing power seems to emanate from the dancer.[23]

According to this rather fanciful interpretation, Ireland retains, in the minds of the revellers, its image as Otherworld island inhabited by supernatural beings.[24]

As for monstrous creatures in Ireland, in Middle English romances we find two Irish dragons: first, the Irish dragon that tears up Northumberland and is finally defeated by Guy of Warwick:

> Þer is comen opon þi lond
> A best þat bringeþ it al to schond.
> Out of Irlond it come;
> To miche harm it haþ y-don.
> It no leueþ man no wiman non,
> Þat it no sleþ hem ichone
> Bot sum þat aschaped beþ
> Þurch chaunce and to þe cites.
> It freteþ men & bestes also;
> Riȝt for soþe y telle þe to,
> Neuer nas beste no so kene.
>
> (ll. 7145–55)

Second, Sir Tristrem, arriving in Ireland to woo Ysonde for his uncle King Mark, finds that a dragon is terrorizing the people of Dublin:

> Out of deuelin toun
> Þe folk wel fast ran
> In awater to droun,
> So ferd were þai þan.
> For doute of o dragoun. . . .
>
> (ll. 1409–13)

Tristrem volunteers to kill the beast somewhat reluctantly—"For nede now wo is me!" (l. 1426)—finally confronts it:

> Helle fere, him pouȝt,
> Fram þat dragoun fleiȝe.
> . . . .
> Wiþ a spere feloun
> He smot him in þe side;
> It no vailed o botoun,
> Oway it gan to glide,
> His dent;
> The deuel dragouns hide
> Was hard so any flint.
>
> (ll. 1439–52)

Tristrem finally defeats this tough and slippery dragon, cuts out its tongue and tucks it "In his hose next the hide" (l. 1486) for safekeeping. He then goes ten paces and collapses, speechless, overcome by the poison in the tongue (ll. 1488–91). Fortunately, he is rescued by the Irish, who revive him by pouring a healing potion down his throat (ll. 1514–20).[25]

In the romances, when Irish people are presented in a positive light, as in *King Horn,* where the Irish king Þurston and his sons help Horn regain his heritage, they appear no more unusual than any romantic character (this motif will be discussed later). When the Irish appear as enemies, however, they are almost always described as giants—again, denizens of the Otherworld. The function of giants in medieval romance has been explored in detail by Darryl F. Lane in his dissertation, "An Historical Study of the Giant in the Middle English Metrical Romances." Lane concludes that the giant

> is invariably evil and inimical to humankind. Often, the giant is associated with narratives of national origin; a race of giants must be defeated before a new culture or country can be established. He also functions as a religious enemy, and must be destroyed by a virtuous champion of Christianity.[26]

Irish giants clearly fulfill one or both of these functions. Some of the earliest examples are found in *Arthoure and Merlin* (1250–1300), in which King Rion of Ireland, is supported by twenty other gigantic, heathen Irish kings who attack London:

> A king hiȝt Leodebron
> And þe king Senigram
> Swiþe fel and wicke man
> And þe king Maudelec
> Þat euer waited scaþe and skec
> And þe king Sernagare,
> Of Yrlond al þai ware;
> Þis four heþen kinges
> Wente to loken þis robbeinges,
> And were so wroþ þat king Arthour
> Hadde ywarnist toun and tour
> Þat þe cuntre about Lounde
> Slowen and brent to þe grounde
> . . . .
> Man and wiif and children bo
> No hadde þai no pite to slo
> Þe folk schirsten so heiȝe and loude
> Þat it schilled into þe cloude.

(ll. 4719–40)

The obvious evil of these merciless kings is emphasized when they are described as "Sarrazins" who swear "by Mahoun" (ll. 4809, 4863), anachronisms that establish them as both national and religious enemies. While Arthur goes to the immediate aid of King Leodegan against King Rion, his knights resist these other giants:

> Ac Wawain swiþe noble was
> For þer he met king Thoas
> A wiʒt geaunt gret and strong
> Of † fet fourtene he was long
> A king he was of Yrlond
>
> .   .   .   .
> Galathin met king Sanigran
> An unsely hoge man
>
> .   .   .   .
> Þo þai seiʒen ich ʒou say
> VIII þousand in o valay
> Of wiche her maister king
> Was yhoten Gvinbating,
> Anoþer hiʒt Medalan
> Boþe wiʒt and hoge man.
> (*Arthoure and Merlin* ll. 4883–87, 4891–92,
>   4999–5004)

The poem goes on for about fifteen hundred lines detailing strenuous battles between Arthur and his knights and all twenty gigantic Irish kings, including King Canlang (fifteen feet tall), King Clarion (fourteen feet tall), King Saphiran, and others (ll. 5697–6430).

King Rion himself seems somewhat to fit the role described by T. McAlindon in his essay on "The Emergence of a Comic Type in Middle English Literature: The Devil and Giant as Buffoon", that of

> a great blunderer, a gluttonous simpleton or interfering bully. . . . Starting with a noisy show of might, and ending in a condition of helplessness. . . .[27]

For example, when Rion hears that his gigantic lieutenants have been defeated by Arthur's knights, he is enraged. He sends "overal into Irlond / And into Danmark also" (ll. 6436–37) for his vassals, and invades England. After about twenty-five hundred lines of preparation and preliminary battles, the two armies face one another. King Rion is described as seventeen feet tall (l. 8975) and very strong and brave. The battle begins, and Rion kills or wounds many knights. His standard is borne by four elephants (again we see the anachronistic association of the Irish with Arabian or North African "Saracens") and when the standard is felled, the Irish army scatters. Rion's first reaction is to kill twenty Christian Englishmen outright, but his men force him to retreat (ll. 9304–14). Then King Rion throws a tantrum, and it is here that we see his ridiculous side:

> Ac fram his men he dassed sone
> Bi a wode oway alone
> Makeand ful sikerly
> Swiþe miche diol and cri.
> Swiche noyse rose in þe bataile
> Þat þei it hadde þondred saun faile
> No schuld men it yhere
> Þe paiens made so rewely bere
> (*Arthoure and Merlin* ll. 9315–22)

A similar, but more elaborate passage in Laȝamon's *Brut* deals with the Irish King Gillomar, defending his country and its Giants' Ring against the depredations of King Uther and the English army. While Gillomar is not specifically stated to be a giant, the kings' similar attitudes and the similarity of the two incidents are difficult to ignore. Also, the fact that in almost every other instance of the Irish as enemies of the English, they *are* described as giants, leads me to believe that this passage is not out of place as an example of a hostile giant reduced to ridiculous helplessness. In this case, the English have arrived in Ireland to capture the "Giants' Ring." King Gillomar hears of it and summons his armies:

> 7 he gone þretien swiðe . þat al he wolde heom to-driue.
> . . . .
> þa þe king Gillomar . makede muc'chel hoker 7 scarn.
> 7 seide þat heo weoren . sotte iueren.
> þat ouer sæ brade . þider weorden iliðene.
> to sechen þer stanes . ase in heore londe neoren nane.
> and swor a Seint Brændan . Ne scullen heo læden ænne stan.
> ah for þan stane heo scullen ibiden . alre baluwen mæst.
> heore blod ȝeoten . ut of heore buken.
> 7 swa me scal heom tachen . stanes to sæchen.
> 7 seoððen ic wulle buȝen . in-to Brut-londe.
> 7 suggen þan king Aurilie . þat mine stanes ich wullen werien.
> 7 buten þe king beon stille . 7 don mine iwille.
> ich wulle in his londe . mid fæhte at-[ston]den.
> maken him west paðes . 7 wildernes modie.

widewen i-noʒe . heore weres scullen deʒe.
Þus þe vnwise king . plaʒede mid worden.
ah al an oðer hit iwærd . oðer he iwende.
ʒaru was hes ferde . 7 forð heo gon fusen.
swa longe þat heo comen . þer læien Brutes on.
To-gaderen heo comen . 7 hærd-liche on-sloʒen.
7 fuhten feond-liche . feollen þa fæie.
Þa Irisce weoren bare . 7 Bruttes iburnede.
þa Irisce fullen . 7 wriʒen al þa feldes.
7 þe king Gillomar . gon him to fleonne þar,
7 flæh for ð-rihtes . mid twenti of his cnihtes.
in-to ænne muchele wude . wurðscipen biræiued.
wes his Irisce uolc . mid stele iualled
Þus wes þe king iscænd . 7 þus he endede his ʒelp.
7 þus to wude ferden . 7 lette his folc fællen.

(II.8631–65)

There is a remarkably Anglo-Saxon flavor in the way the poem contrasts Gillomar's scornful threats ("his ʒelp") with his disgraceful abandonment of his men as he flees from the field. We may compare this passage with similar commentary in Old English works such as *The Battle of Maldon*.[28] (Considering the early date of the *Brut* [ca. 1225], perhaps this is not so remarkable.) A similar incident is described later, in which this same Gillomar allies himself with Passent against Uther, and although the fighting is fierce, he hangs back from the battle until shamed by his men into joining.

Þa iseʒen Irisce men . þat Brutten wes an eornest .
feond-liche he fuhten . and neoðeles heo feollen .
heo cleopeden on heore king . Whar ært þu niðing .
whi nult þu hiðer wenden . þu lezst us her schenden .
and Passent þin ifere . i-sih us fallen here .
cumeð us to halpe . mid hahʒere strengðe .
Þis ihered Gillomar . þer-foren was his heorte sær .
mid his Irisce cnihten . he com to þan fihte .

(Laʒamon II.9018–25)

Another example of the giant king as bully occurs in Malory's *Morte Darthur* (ca. 1470). Here called "Kynge Royns of North Walis, and kynge he was of all Irelonde and of Iles," he sends the following message to King Arthur:

gretynge well Kyng Arthure on thys maner of wyse, sayng that kyng Royns had discomfite and overcom eleven kyngis, and every one of them dud hym omage. And that was thus to say they gaff theire beardes clene flayne off, as much as was bearde; wherefore the messyngere com for kynge Arthures berde. For kyng Royns had purfilde a mantell with kynges berdis, and there lacked one place of the mantell; wherefore he sente for hys bearde, othir ellis he wolde entir into his londis and brenne and sle, and nevir leve tylle he hathe the hede and the bearde bothe. . . . (Malory, 36–37)

Naturally, Arthur refuses; Royns invades England, is roundly defeated, and ends by giving homage to Arthur. The *Prose Merlin* (ca. 1450) contains the same story, except that in this version, Rion wants Arthur's beard merely for "tassels" to trim his cloak made of king's beards (III.625).

In the alliterative *Morte Arthure*, the Irish are among Arthur's opponents, and are closely associated with Scottish giants and with "Picts and pagans":

> Ethyns of Argayle and Irische kynges
> Enverounes oure avawmewarde with venymos berynes;
> Peghttes and paynymes with perilous wapyns
>
> . . . .
>
> Sir Ewayne and sir Errakes, thes excellente beryns,
> Enters in one the oste, and egerly strykes,
> The ethynys of Orkkenaye and Irische kynges
>
> (ll. 4123–25, 4161–63)

Yet another Irish giant is Sir Tristrem's opponent, Sir Moraunt, "a neten" (*Sir Tristrem* l. 950); he also wields a poisoned sword. The battle between the giant Sir Moraunt and Sir Tristrem generally follows the pattern previously described: a boastful challenge from the seemingly indestructible giant, who, when he realizes that Sir Tristrem is winning, reveals his vulnerability:

> Tristrem him self ʒede
> Moraunt word to bring,
> And schortliche seyd in lede:—
> "We no owe þe noþing."
> Moraunt oʒain sede:—
> "Þou lexst afoule lesing!
> Mi body to batayl y bede
> To proue bi for þe king
> To loke."
> He waged him aring,
> Tristrem þe batayl toke.
>
> . . . .
>
> Þe yland was ful brade

þat þai gun in fiȝt;
Þer of was moraunt glade,
Of tristrem he lete liȝt.

. . . .

Riȝt þo
In moräuntes most nede
His stede bak brak on to.
Vp he stirt in drede
And seyd:—"tristrem, aliȝt,
For þou hast slayn mi stede.
A fot þou schalt fiȝt."

(*Sir Tristrem* ll. 1002–12, 1024–27, 1054–60)

Tristrem meets every challenge, however, and finally slays Moraunt by a blow to the head that breaks his sword, leaving a shard in Moraunt's brain. The author emphasizes the nationalistic element of this conflict by beseeching "God help tristrem þe kniȝt! / He fauȝt for ingland" (ll. 1033–34) and by Tristrem's warning to the Irish spectators:

"Folk of yrland side,
ȝour mirour ȝe may se.
Mo þat hider wil ride,
Þus grayþed schul ȝe be."

(ll. 1092–95)

A nongigantic parallel to this passage may be seen in the conflict between two of King Arthur's knights in Malory. Sir Balin kills a lady in front of the whole court, and King Arthur banishes him for it.

So at that tyme there was a knyght, the which was the kynges son of Irelonde, and hys name was Launceor, the which was an orgulus knyght and accompted hymselff one of the beste of the courte. And he had grete despite at Balyne for the enchevynge of the swerde, that ony sholde be accompted more hardy or more of prouesse, and he asked kynge Arthure licence to ryde afftir Balyne and to revenge the despite that he had done. (Malory, "Balin" 42)

King Arthur grants permission, and Launceor challenges Balin to single combat, which Balin wins, killing Sir Launceor. Unlike the combat in *Sir Tristrem,* however, Balin is not clearly in the right—first he had indeed behaved unchivalrously (to say the least) in killing a lady, even though she was "the untrwyste lady lyvynge, and by inchauntement . . . the destroyer of many good knyghtes," as Sir Balin told King Arthur after her death (Malory, "Balin" 41); and second, Balin must repent for killing Sir Launceor as well, when the dead knight's lady arrives and kills herself in sorrow for her lover (Malory, "Balin" 43).

Gigantic or not, the Irish appear over and over again in the romances as hostile invaders ultimately repulsed by the English. One notable example in which there is no suggestion that the Irish are extraordinary is the invasion of three Irish kings, in *Horn Childe:*

> Out of yrlond com kinges þre,
> Her names can y telle þe,
>   Wele wiþ outen les:
> Ferwele & winwald were þer to,
> Malkan king was on of þo,
>   Proude in ich apres;
> Al westmer land stroyed þay.

(ll. 148–54)

Horn at this time is in the service of King Haþeolf, who is really the star of this battle in which the Irish outnumber the English greatly:

> Þe irise host was long & brade,
> On staines more þer þai rade,
>   Þai ʒaf a crie for prede;
> Hende haþeolf hem abade,
> Swiche meting was neuer made,
>   Wiþ sorwe on ich aside;
> . . . .
> King haþeolf slouʒ wiþ his hond,
> Þat was comen out of yrlond,
>   Tvo kinges þat tide.
> King haþeolf was wel wo,
> For þe irise host was mani & mo
>   Wiþ sheld & wiþ spere;
> . . . .
> Þei king haþeolf fauʒt fast,
> King malkan stiked attelast
>   His stede þat schuld him bere;
> Now schal men finde kinges fewe,
> Þat in batail be so trewe,
>   His lond forto were.

When king haþeolf on fot stode,
Þe yrise folk about him ȝode,
   As hondes do to bare;
Whom he hit opon þe hode,
Were he neuer kniȝt so gode,
   He ȝaue a dint wel sare;
He brouȝt in alitel stounde
Wel fif þousende to grounde
   Wiþ his grimly gare.
Þe Irise ost tok hem to red,
To ston þat douhti kniȝt to ded,
   Þai durst neiȝe him na mare.

Gret diol it was to se
Of hende haþeolf þat was so fre,
   Stones to him þai cast;
Þai brak him boþe legge & kne,
Gret diol it was to se,
   He kneled attelast.
King malcan wiþ wretþe out stert
& smot king haþeolf to þe hert;
   He held his wepen so fast,
Þat king malkan smot his arm atvo,
Er he miȝt gete his swerd him fro,
   For nede his hert tobrast.

Þo king malkan wan þe priis,
Oway brouȝt he no mo ywis,
   Of his men bot þritten,
Þat wounded were in bak & side;
Þai fleiȝe & durst nouȝt abide,
   Daþet, who him be mene!
To yrlond he com oȝain,
& left her fair folk al slain
   Lieand on þe grene.

                    (ll. 181–237)

We can see in this passage the nationalistic emphasis on the bravery and prowess of King Haþeolf—"Now schal men finde kinges fewe, / Þat in batail be so trewe, / His lond forto were" (ll. 202–4), contrasted with the churlish behavior of the Irish in stoning him to death because they are afraid to get close to him (ll. 214–22). They surround him "as hondes do to bere" (l. 207). The author also contrasts the courage of Haþeolf with the cowardice of the Irish king Malkan, who only approaches the English king after he has been felled by the soldiers' stones, and even after Malkan thrusts his sword into Haþeolf's heart, Haþeolf apparently grips the sword so tightly that Malkan must cut Haþeolf's arm off in order to get it back (ll. 220–27).

Ireland as Wilderness/Refuge

In certain other romances, Ireland serves as simply a wild wasteland, not necessarily supernatural. Giraldus's first description of the island falls into this category.

> Ireland is a country of uneven surface and rather mountainous. The soil is soft and watery, and there are many woods and marshes. Even at the tops of high and steep mountains you will find pools and swamps. Still there are, here and there, some fine plains, but in comparison with the woods they are indeed small. One the whole the land is low-lying on all sides and along the coast; but futher inland it rises up very high to many hills and even high mountains. It is sandy rather than rocky, not only on its circumference, but also in the very interior. (*History* 34)[29]

This view of Ireland as wasteland is also reflected in Louelich's *Merlin,* in which a messenger tells Arthur of an attack on his ally King Leodegan by the Irish "kyng Ryown of Geawntez / and of wildernesse, that fewe men hawntez" (II.8205–6), combining the Otherworldly element of giants with the wilderness motif.[30]

Though the wasteland may harbor dangers, it sometimes is the equivalent of the biblical desert—a place of safe exile for those fleeing enemies at home. For example, in the *Alliterative Morte Arthure* (c. 1400) Mordred, fearing Arthur's revenge for his marrying Guenevere,

> Bade hir ferkene oo ferre, and fflee with hir childire,
> Whills he myghte wile hyme awaye, and wyne to hire speche,
> Ayere in-to Irelande, in-to thas owte-mowntes,
> And wonne thare in wilderness with-in tha wast landys
>
> (ll.3907–10)

(Guinevere does not take this advice, however, but instead seeks sanctuary in a nunnery.) Compare this image of Ireland as a refuge to instances of historical figures who were out of favor in England, such as Piers Gaveston and supporters of the Yorkist faction, who were forced to go to Ireland for a time.[31]

Ireland also serves as a place of exile, but not necessarily a wasteland, in *King Horn* (ca. 1225). Horn, the rightful heir to Westernesse, flees to Ireland from the enemy who has usurped his throne:

> To hauene he [him] ferde
> A god schup he [him] h[er]de
> Þat him scholde l[e]fde
> [Vt of Westernesse þede];
> [Þe whyȝt him gan wel stonde]
> [And drof to Irlonde]
>
> (*King Horn* ll. 769–74)

The Irish as Allies

The Irish appear as the hero's allies occasionally in Middle English romances: the two most notable examples are *King Horn* and one episode of *Horn Childe* (c. 1320), and, as mentioned earlier, there is nothing Otherwordly about them. In *King Horn* it is the Irish (under King Þurston) who are threatened by a giant "iarmed of paynyme" (l.821). Horn, otherwise known as Cutberd,[32] volunteers to fight this giant singlehandedly, saying that one Christian ought to be more than equal to even a gigantic pagan. The giant's revelation that he killed Horn's father, King Murry, and the memory of Rimenhilde give Horn the enraged strength to kill the giant. In the ensuing general melée, King Þurston's sons Harild and Berild are killed, so the King offers his kingdom and his daughter's hand in marriage to Horn. Horn, however, remains faithful to Rimenhilde and politely declines (ll.887–936).

In a later episode of *King Horn*, Horn, still in the service of King Þurston, sails to war against the land of Suddenne, leading a host of Irish warriors, one of whom is described as "Aþulf wiþ him his brother: / Nolde he [habbe] non oþer" (ll. 1321–22). In other words, this Aþulf is like a brother to him. When they arrive in Suddenne, Horn boasts:

> Iblessed beo þe time
> I com [in]to Suddenne
> Wiþ min irisse men!
> [Þis lond we schulle winne]
> And [sle þat þer beþ inne]:
> We schulle þe hundes teche
> To speken vre speche.
>
> (ll. 1396–1402)

Horn Childe is set primarily in England, but following the invasion of Irish kings mentioned earlier, King Finlak, another Irish king, asks the new English king Houlac for help against the Irish King Malkan. Horn is the leader this time, and avenges the death of his lord Haþeolf by killing Malkan. King Finlak's two sons die in the battle, so he offers his kingdom and his daughter Acula to Horn, who politely declines, remaining faithful to Rimnild (ll. 682–840)—an episode obviously parallel to the one just mentioned from *King Horn*.

In several Arthurian romances, the Irish, once conquered, become Arthur's loyal allies in his later campaigns. In Laȝamon's *Brut,* for example, King Arthur finally defeats and captures Gillomar, but treats him with respect and offers friendship. Gillomar repents, swears fealty to Arthur, and offers him tribute, including "sume sixti" children as fosterlings (II.11,168–69) and a variety of Christian relics:

> halidom .
> of seint Columkille . þe dude Godes iwille .
> 7 seint Brændenes hæfed . þe Godd seolf haleȝede .
> 7 seint Bride riht fot . pe hali is 7 swiðe god
>
> (II.11,178–81)

After this, Arthur calls on his Irish allies several times. Gillomar joins his attack on France with eleven thousand men (II.11,655–63), and is present at a great feast in "Kairliun," by which time, it seems, his people have forgiven him his poor showing earlier, for he is called "Irisce monnen deorling" (II.12,166). The Irish also support Arthur's invasion of Italy (II.12,686). On the other hand, Mordred also recruits help from Ireland as he prepares his rebellion (II.14,217–24).

The Irish, or some of them, also appear as King Arthur's allies in other romances. For example, in the *Alliterative Morte Arthure,* Ireland is listed among the many countries that Arthur has conquered (ll. 26–48) and who pay him tribute (ll. 2357–60). The *Stanzaic Morte Arthure* (late fourteenth century) and Malory also include the Irish among Arthur's allies (*Le Morte Arthure* ll. 2094–2101; Malory 229–624). Lovelich's *History of the Holy Grail* says that Sir Lancelot "weddid A kynges dowhter Of Irlonde" (IV.348, l. 257). Lovelich also says, regarding "Mordret":

> Kyng Arthur On his Soster Engendred hym
> As Manye bokys it telleth In Rym;

For he wende the Maiden of Yrland it hadde be,
whanne that to his Soster wente he"
                (*History of the Holy Grail* chap. LII, ll.1147–50)

This may be another reference to an Irish Guinevere (cf. *Sir Launfal*)—in other words, Arthur mistook his sister for his betrothed (either by accident or by her magic arts, as some tales have it)—but Lovelich never explicitly identifies King Arthur's wife as Irish.

The Irish as Friends: *Sir Tristrem* and Malory's "Book of Sir Tristram of Lyones"

In both *Sir Tristrem* and Malory's "Book of Sir Tristram of Lyones," the Irish first appear as hostile, with their demand for "truage" from King Mark of Cornwall that includes not only gold and silver, but children as well (*Sir Tristrem* ll. 931–52); in Malory the tribute is not specified, except that it is seven years overdue (231), which puts Mark somewhat in the wrong. However, once Sir Tristram actually arrives in Ireland, both versions of the tale present a generally positive view of the Irish, in spite of the gigantic Sir Moraunt (or Marhalt), the dragon, and the magic potion and poisoned weapon mentioned before (Malory omits the dragon). These elements, along with Tristram's voyage in an unguided boat (*Sir Tristrem* ll. 1160–66), may suggest an Otherworldly Ireland, yet Sir Tristram is for the most part treated well there, and Ysonde (or La Beale Isoude) is a pleasant reward for his trials, although their love is doomed.

In both versions the Irish, finding a wounded stranger (Tristram) in a boat, take him in and care for him until he recovers. They then treat him as an honored guest, although they know nothing of his background. Even when comparison of his broken sword (left in the dragon he kills in *Sir Tristrem;* lying in his room in Malory) with the fragment from Sir Moraunt's mortal wound reveals that the stranger (in Malory, he calls himself "Tramtryste" [238]) is Tristrem who killed Ysonde's kinsman, Tristrem is able to talk her out of killing him—she is not an unreasonable barbarian (*Sir Tristrem* ll. 1231–1643). In Malory's version (238–44), it is the Irish queen who wants to kill Sir Tristram, but the Irish king forbids her. He then goes to "sir Tramtryste" and says:

". . . thus muche I shall do for my worshyp and for thy love: in so muche as thou arte wythin my courte, hit were no worship to sle the;

> therefore upon this conducion I woll gyff the leve for to departe frome this courte in savyté, so thou wolte tell me who was thy fadir and what is thy name, and also yf thou slewe sir Marhalte, my brother." (242)

Tristram then offers to defend himself in single combat against anyone in the Irish court whom he may have offended by killing Sir Marhalt. "And all they stood stylle—there was nat one that wolde sey one worde. Yett were there som knyghtes that wer of the quenys bloode and of sir Marhaltys blood, but they wold nat meddyll wyth hym" (244)—perhaps because they all know he is the best knight in the country. These courtly Irish people are far from the treacherous barbarians described in Higden's *Polychronicon* (citing Giraldus). Though I would like to argue that Thomas Malory had a higher opinion of the Irish than many Englishmen of his time, it seems more likely that Ireland in this tale owes more to such mythical countries as "Lyonesse"—simply part of Malory's imaginary chivalrous geography. Malory's portrayal of Ireland may also owe largely to his French source, which would undoubtedly have been less biased against Ireland.

However, in both versions, one element that is typical of the "real" Ireland is the importance of music. Even Giraldus Cambrensis had acknowledged (somewhat grudgingly), "It is only in the case of musical instruments that I find any commendable diligence in the [Irish] people. They seem to me to be incomparably more skilled in these than any other people that I have seen" (*History* 103). Tristram's musical ability wins him early acceptance in Ireland.

> And at hys aryvayle he sate and harped in his bedde a merry lay: such one herde they never none in Irelonde before that tyme. And whan hit was told the kynge and the quene of such a syke knyght that was suche an harper, anone the kynge sent for him and lette serche hys woundys, and than he asked hym his name. (Malory 238)

Sir Tristrem, recovering from his fight with the dragon under the care of the Irish queen, becomes quite a celebrity in the Irish court:

> He made his play aloft,
> His gamnes he gan kiþe,
> For þi was tristrem oft
> To boure cleped fele siþe
> To sete;
> Ich man was lef to liþe,
> His mirþes were so swete.
>
> (*Sir Tristrem* ll. 1248–54)

Music also brings Tristram and Ysonde together: in Malory, "Tramtryste lerned hir to harpe and she began to have a grete fantasy unto hym" (259). In *Sir Tristrem,* Ysonde is already a skilled musician, but Tristrem is even better, and becomes her tutor:

> Ysonde of heiȝe priis
>
> . . . .
> In warld was non so wiis
> Of craft þat men knewe
> Wiþ outen sir tramtris
>
> . . . .
> Ysonde he dede vnder stand
> What alle playes were
> In lay.
>
> (ll. 1266–72, 1283–85)

The Romances as Historical Evidence

It is difficult, if not impossible, to make explicit connections between statements or implied attitudes about Ireland in the romances and actual contemporary history. The often uncertain dating of the manuscripts, the still more uncertain dating of the texts themselves, and the nature of the material all make attempts to attach historical relevance risky and possibly irrelevant. Occasionally one encounters a suggestion that a certain work reflects contemporary historical or political persons or events. Valerie Krishna details the ambiguities of one such analysis in her edition of the alliterative *Morte Arthure.*

> Neilson, who regards Edward III as the model for Arthur and the poem as a criticism of the Hundred Years' War, suggests the date 1365, which has gained wide acceptance. . . . Finlayson . . . shows that a number of the [historical references] are found in the Chandos Herald's *Life of the Black Prince,* written in 1385.[33]

As Krishna points out, the possibility of a later date does not necessarily preclude the poem being a criticism of the Hundred Years' War, but this is the kind of problem one is faced with in attempting to connect romances to contemporary history.

The figure of King Arthur, however, "from the very beginning . . . had strong political implications," according to Karl Heinz Göller.

This was already true of Geoffrey of Monmouth's *Historia Regum Britanniae,* which saw King Arthur as an incarnation of the idea of the Empire. Most English kings after the conquest have regarded themselves as lawful heirs and successors of King Arthur. An entire series of kings had no objections against being styled as Arturus redivivus. Henry III led his troops under the Arthurian banner of the dragon. Edward I was an "Arthurian enthusiast" and held jousts and tournaments which he called "Table Rounds". The same is true of Edward III, the founder of the Order of the Garter. . . .

John Lydgate called Henry V "of knyhthode Lodesterre, . . . Able to stond among the worthy nyne", which recalls King Arthur as the most famous of the Worthies.[34]

Thus it must be relevant that the conquest of Ireland by King Arthur is included in every Middle English romance account of his reign.

Numerous passages in romances may very well draw on actual elements of Irish culture and history recorded in Latin and Middle English chronicles and in other sources, possibly even Irish sources. I prefer not to comment on the intentionality of such references, but will point out those that seem analogous to what we know of actual medieval Irish culture and history.

For example, the importance of music in Irish culture has already been mentioned in the discussion of *Sir Tristrem* and "The Tale of Sir Tristram." Another reference that may reflect at least one writer's knowledge of a typical feature of Irish culture is in the *Prose Merlin* (ca. 1450–60), where King Riolent of Ireland (also called Rion) is described as "Kyng of the londe of Geauntes and of the londe of pastures" (I.114). Giraldus Cambrensis had noted, "The island is . . . richer in pastures than in crops, and in grass than in grain" (*History* 34). The description of Ireland in a later source, the *Polychronicon* (Trevisa's Middle English translation) quotes Giraldus, and adds a passage from Solinus.

> Þere is grete plente of noble pasture and of lese; þerfore bestes moot ofte be dreue out of hir lese, lest þey fede hem self to ful and schende hemself, and þey moste ete at hir owne wille. (I.333)

Similarly, Giraldus had described (disapprovingly) how the Irish people live. "They have not progressed at all from the primitive habits of pastoral living. . . . They use the fields generally as pasture, but pasture in poor condition" (*History* 101–2), a passage paraphrased by Higden/Trevisa as "þese men forsakeþ tilienge of lond and kepeþ pasture for beestes" (I.353).

The early Irish sagas and law tracts contain numerous references to cows, cattle-herding, and cattle-raiding (e.g., *Táin Bó Cuailnge* [*The Cattle Raid of Cooley*] and the law tract *Críth Gablach*), suggesting that cattle played a fundamental role in Irish economy and society. Studies of later medieval Irish culture also note that "[l]ife for most [Irish] people revolved around the stock, and herding cattle and moving them from place to place was a widespread custom";[35] and, "[g]iven Ireland's abundance of grass, the reliance on cattle-rearing is hardly surprising."[36]

In Middle English romances, Ireland and the Irish are often identified with medieval Scandinavian territory and culture. It is certainly true that in the ninth and tenth centuries the Vikings, after raiding the northern and eastern Irish coasts, set up colonies there—Dublin was one—from whence they could more conveniently raid the British coasts. These colonies maintained their ties with Norway and Denmark and their territories in the northern British Isles (the Orkneys, e.g.) for many years. As mentioned in chapter 2, these Viking raiders are often identified as "Scots," that is, Irish, in Anglo-Saxon texts.

It seems unlikely that Middle English readers (or writers) would have been aware of this. The sources for the earlier history of Ireland available to them, such as Giraldus and the *Polychronicon,* make little mention of Scandinavian settlers in their accounts of the settlement of Ireland (*History* 120, 121; *Polychronicon* 347–51), though there are numerous references to alliances between the Irish and the Saxons in such chronicles as *Brut* (Laȝamon and *Prose Brut*), Robert Mannyng of Brunne's *Story of England,* and Robert of Gloucester's *Metrical Chronicle*. In one passage from the *Polychronicon* that almost certainly refers to raiders from the Norse settlements in Ireland, they are simply identified as Irish. "Also þis yere Irische men were robbours on þe see, and entred into þe see of Severne, and wiþ the help of Gryffyn, king of Wales, þey dede moche robberie about þe water of Vaga" (VI.xxiii).[37] Giraldus had described the invasions and settlements of the Vikings ("Ostmen") in his *Historia et Topographia Hibernica* (*History* 117), but Higden seems to have omitted this passage.

But in the romances, especially Arthurian tales, we find frequent associations of, or references to alliances between, Ireland and the Norse colonies in northern Britain—the Orkneys, Argyle, Galloway, and so forth—and even with Norway and Denmark:

> The kynge comly over-kest knyghtes and othire,
>
> . . . .
>
> Of Orgaile and Orekenay, the Iresche kynges,
> The nobilieste of Norwaye, nowmbirs fulle hugge,
> Dukes of Danamarkes . . .
>> (*Alliterative Morte Arthure* ll. 3932–36, cf. ll. 26–48, 3532)

One reference to King Rion in the *Prose Merlin* calls him "the kynge Rion of Denmarke and of Irelonde" (II.228). Lovelich's *Merlin* describes an Irish king with a part-Norse name and Danish connections:

> Antref Maglaans, that hethen wernlyng,
> which that kyng was of jrlond
> and cosyn germain, as j vndirstond,
> To that riche kyng þat of Denmarke was,
> and king hostelices broþer, so happed his cas;
> which ostelyce hadde jn gouernaunce tho
> a gret part of Denmark and of Yrlond also
>> (III.460)

According to the *Romans of Partenay* (ca. 1500), those who trace their lineage to the characters Melusine and Lusignan include both Norwegians and Irish:

> Off tho knyghtes ben yut, lo! in Norway,
>
> . . . .
>
> And knowyn ouerall ryght openly
> That they discended be of þat line hy
> Off lusignan, which is notable grett,
> Which so issued, into yrlande gett,
>
> And vnto many Another contre,
> As beforne is said by our gouernaill
>> (ll. 6280–88)

One of the earliest, and most unusual examples, of course, is *King Horn* (c. 1225), in which the major Irish characters not only have Norse names—King Þurston and his sons Harild and Barild—but are also the hero's allies, in contrast with examples cited previously, in which the Irish/Norse are enemies of English heroes. In short, Middle English romances seem to have preserved, perhaps unintentionally, elements of Irish (and British) history generally passed over by contemporary historians.

4

Ireland and the Irish in Saints' Lives

In the earliest days of Christianity in the British Isles, evangelical influences went first from Britain to Ireland. Gearóid Mac Niocaill cites linguistic evidence for the early diffusion of Christianity from Romano-Celtic Britain into Ireland:

> the vocabulary of this new religion [in Ireland] was borrowed either from British or from Latin pronounced in the British fashion—such terms as *cáisc* "Easter", *cruimthir* "priest", *caille* "veil", *fescor* "vespers", and *sléchtad* "prostration, bowing down", made their way into primitive Irish no later than the fifth century, before it evolved into archaic Old Irish. British slaves captured in raids are one possible channel of entry, and contacts mediated by the Irish colonies in Britain are another.[1]

St. Patrick, of course, first came to Ireland as a slave, and later returned as a missionary. After the pagan Anglo-Saxons conquered Celtic Britain, Irish Christians returned the evangelical favor through missionaries such as St. Aidan, who is also frequently mentioned in Anglo-Saxon sources.

The early evangelistic efforts from Celtic Britain to Ireland had mainly influenced "details of monastic organization, discipline and the forms of the liturgy" (Mac Niocaill 24)[2]—details which distinguished the church in Ireland and Wales from the more Roman-influenced Continental and English churches for centuries, and which Rome increasingly viewed as at best misguided, at worst heretical. Even after the Irish church began to reshape itself to conform more with Roman practice, its reputation for questionable discipline remained, and was used as an excuse for the Anglo-Norman church to take more control of Irish church affairs, as will be discussed in more detail later. Nevertheless, before the devastating Viking raids of the ninth and tenth centuries, Irish monks had gained a far-reaching reputation for erudition and sanctity in England and on the Continent; even after the Vikings had disrupted the system in Ireland, exiled Irish monks in Europe were known for their high standard of learning.

The Venerable Bede, in *Historia Ecclesiastica Gentis Anglorum,* describes the role of Irish missionaries in the conversion of the English (227, 269–77, passim), cites many remarkably pious Irish clerics, and writes admiringly of the Irish monks' hospitality and love of learning. For example, he tells how, in the midseventh century

> there were many in England, both nobles and commons, who, in the days of Bishops Finan and Colman, had left their own country and retired to Ireland either for the sake of religious studies or to live a more ascetic life. In course of time some of these devoted themselves faithfully to the monastic life, while others preferred to travel round to the cells of various teachers and apply themselves to study. The Irish welcomed them all gladly, gave them their daily food, and also provided them with books to read and with instruction, without asking for any payment.[3]

But Bede also describes in great detail the distressing controversy over the method used by the Irish church to determine the date for celebrating Easter, quoting several letters from bishops and popes urging the "Scots" to follow the method approved by the church of Rome (147, 199–201, 533–53). At last, early in the eighth century, the last of the Irish foundations which had upheld the old method adopted the new system (Bede, 553–55).

This "reform," though not reversed, was overshadowed by the devastating Viking raids that began soon afterward and continued over the next two hundred years. By the eleventh century, Irish monastic churches had become, in effect, secular organizations. Both Irish and non-Irish churchmen began to recognize that in matters of marriage and divorce Irish "native law had triumphed over the stricter provisions of the church" and that the Irish method of consecrating bishops was at variance with Roman practice.[4] James F. Kenny notes, "The marriage of ecclesiastics, both clergy and lay monks, and the attraction of the church property, were secularising forces at work in Ireland as on the Continent,"[5] but because of the peculiar "exernal forms and circumstances"[6] of the Irish monastic system, Continental and Anglo-Norman reformers, inspired by the Cluniac movement (which began in tenth-century France), saw the situation in Ireland as much more depraved than it actually was. But the Irish themselves were well aware of the deficiencies of their church, as Kenny points out.

Inspiration, advice, example may have come from abroad, but the driving force which effected the ecclesiastical revolution of the twelfth century came from within the Irish Church. These Irish reformers had three tasks before them. . .: the first was to bring the organisation and exernal forms of the Church into uniformity with that of the Continent; the second was to abolish the abuses—evils from both the Irish and the foreign point of view—which had grown up; and the third was to improve the morality and spirituality of the people.[7]

J. A. Watt, in *The Church and the Two Nations in Medieval Ireland,* defines three major periods of this Irish reform movement: its beginnings in the late eleventh century; the vigorous changes that took place under the influence of St. Malachy of Armagh, from 1119 to 1148; and, most decisive, the edicts of the Council of Kells-Mellifont in 1152.[8] A few years later, in 1166, the rebellion of Dermot MacMurrough set off the first round of the Anglo-Norman invasion of Ireland. Its effect on the reform movement (as on Irish society in general) was "essentially disruptive" states Watt.

It was possible to argue that Angevin lordship of Ireland would advance Church reform and accelerate its progress. At any rate, Popes Adrian IV and Alexander III endorsed this argument and the Irish hierarchy initially acquiesced in it. . . . [But] the eventual consequence was the emergence of a division between the Church *inter Hibernicos* and the Church *inter Anglicos.* The antagonism of these sections ensured that Ireland remained throughout the middle ages what possibly by the turn of mid-twelfth century it was beginning to cease to be, a remote and backward province of the Church, stunted in its growth, distorted in its development.[9]

Watt points out that Henry II's conquest of Ireland "was not primarily a religious crusade. But it might be allowed that he saw the tactical possibilities of exploiting a position as a champion of the Church in the diplomacy that was to come with Pope Alexander III in the aftermath of the Becket murder."[10]

Even before Henry II's political conquest, however, the English church had already seen "tactical possibilities" in their relations with the Irish church. Although, as Kenney states, "on the whole, from the end of the Easter Controversy to the Norman Conquest, eccesiastical relations between Ireland and England were friendly [and] no spirit of aggression towards their brethren beyond St. George's Channel was displayed by English churchmen,"[11] certain English monastic foundations and churches had long attracted Irish pilgrimage trade en route to Europe by promoting the veneration of popular Irish saints, especially during the pre-Norman period.[12] As late as 700, many English were attracted to Ireland for study and religious discipline (Bede 195), but the Irish reputation for scholarship had waned by the twelfth century, judging by William of Malmesbury's comment in his *Memorials of St. Dunstan.* "The Irish today promise great things of their knowledge of language and grammar, but the truth is that they are less than safe guides to the formation of Latin words and the proper speaking of Latin."[13] The Irish church, viewing exile or wandering as a form of holy martyrdom,[14] sent a steady trickle of pilgrims via England to European monasteries and shrines well into the twelfth century.

After the Norman Conquest of England, Anglo-Norman efforts to exert more definite influence over the Irish church became pronounced. In 1070 William the Conqueror nominated Lanfranc of Bec as Archbishop of Canterbury, who then "effected an energetic but fruitful, though unsympathetic, reorganisation of the English Church, and, further, proceeded to assert his supremacy . . . over the whole of Britain and Ireland."[15] In fact, argues Marie Therese Flanagan,

> It is possible that claims to quasi-imperial authority on behalf of the Norman kings were actively fostered at Canterbury as a correlative to Canterbury's own claims to primacy, which were thought to derive support from the *imperium* of the old English kings.[16]

It seems that some reform-minded Irish clerics did in fact look to Canterbury as "a guiding impulse for religious reform . . . notably under Archbishops Lanfranc (1070–89) and Anselm (1093–1109)"[17] and several Irish bishops of Dublin, Waterford, and Limerick went to Canterbury for consecration between 1074 and 1140.[18] And certainly, "the alliance of the clergy was a solid and important fact" in the Anglo-Norman conquest of Ireland, as Otway-Ruthven points out in her *History of Medieval Ireland.*

> [I]n September [1174] pope Alexander III, replying to the letters of the prelates after the council of Cashel, addressed three letters to the archbishops and bishops of Ireland. In the first two the pope referred to the enormities and crimes, the abominable foulness of the Irish, which he had learnt from the letters of the Irish prelates themselves, and from the verbal report of the archdeacon of Llandaff, who, as we saw, had been present at Cashel. The bishops were commanded to assist Henry in maintaining possession of the land, and in extirpating these abominations, visiting with the censures of the church any king, prince, or other person breaking his oath of fealty to Henry; Henry

was congratulated and urged to show still greater energy in the reforming work so laudably begun . . . [T]hese letters were most probably brought over by William fitz Audelm in March or April 1175, and published at the synod of Waterford.[19]

In the early thirteenth century, during the reign of Henry III, the English church instructed "that in future no Irishman should be elected to any see in Ireland since, it was claimed, the promotion of native clergy had very frequently led to unrest. . . . [Instead] only Anglici should be promoted."[20] Rome disapproved of this policy, but there were ways to implement it without attracting Rome's attention. States Watt, "Anglicization of personnel was the essential precondition of any anglicization of institutions and practices."[21]

A more benign approach to English influence over the Irish church was to promote the veneration of Irish saints in England, thus attracting the Irish pilgrimage trade, and also, perhaps, strengthening ties between English and Irish foundations devoted to the same saints. Three types of evidence for the veneration of Irish saints in England are churches and chapels dedicated to a saint or claiming to preserve a saint's relics;[22] inclusion of a saint's feast day in liturgical calendars;[23] and extant manuscripts containing the saint's life. It is with the Middle English vernacular hagiography that we are most concerned here. From all three types of evidence just cited, it seems clear that the Anglo-Saxon church had been more aware than the Anglo-Norman church of "the geographical nearness [and] the historical indebtedness of the English to the Irish church."[24]

Irish Saints in Medieval English Hagiography

In the English church after the Norman Conquest, both clerical and lay English interest in Irish saints seems to fall off considerably. Regarding the evidence of celebration of Irish saints' feast days in the later Middle Ages, John Hennig writes:

Only St. Brigid's feast was celebrated throughout the Middle Ages in all parts of the English Church. St. Patrick's feast disappeared by the twelfth century to be revived, to some extent, in the general expansion of the calendar shortly before the Reformation. St. Aidan was commemorated intermittently down to the fourteenth century; St. Fursey, Columba, Columbanus and Brendan were mentioned in only a few calendars.[25]

This does not mean that other Irish saints were unknown in England during the Middle English period. As Hennig points out in another article,

> In the *Sanctilogium Angliae, Walliae, Scotiae, et Hiberniae* written during the second quarter of the fourteenth century by John of Tynemouth, apparently from English sources largely perused at St. Alban's (the abbey to which Tynemouth belonged), we have lives of SS. Fursey, Brigid, Aed of Ferns, Kieran of Saighir, Patrick, Brendan, Columba, Fiacre, Foillan, Malachy, Columban, Finian of Moville (and many others, in the calendaris order.) . . ."[26]

However, Hennig argues that the inclusion of most of these Irish saints can be traced to their associations with English or Welsh traditions[27] and that, in any case, the *Sanctilogium* "is not a record of a naturally grown legendary of saints actually venerated. It is rather a systematic collection of records of 'saints' . . . without regard to their actual cultus."[28]

Exceptions are found where certain English abbeys had particular interest in strengthening ties with their Irish branches or in attracting Irish pilgrims. For example, Canterbury, a major center of English pilgrimage and an obvious stop on the road to the Continent from Ireland,[29] was well-known for its veneration of St. Fursey and kept a famous relic of the saint: "caput sancti Fursei in capite argenteo deaurato" (the head of St. Fursa in a silver vessel decorated with gold).[30] Records from Worcester, Evesham, and Ramsey give evidence for a variety of contacts with Ireland and visits from Irish pilgrims.[31] In the late twelfth-century calendar of St. Werburgh's Benedictine abbey in Chester (on the Welsh border, and another stopping place for Irish *peregrini* en route to the Continent), an entry for

> "Sancti Patricii archiepiscopi hibernensium apostoli" . . . has been ascribed by Wormald to the gift made to that abbey by John de Courcy of some land in Down in order to build there an abbey of St. Patrick. This association also accounts for the presence in this calendar of the *Inventio corporum sanctorum Patricii, Columbae et Brigidae* on 24th March (clearly the octave of St. Patrick's feast). In contrast to the *Translatio* of these relics, the *Inventio* was not a feast in Ireland. Also the commemoration of St. Columba was added in deference to de Courcy's attempt to bring Irish devotion to the national saints in line with the devotion to the saints in England and on the Continent rather than in deference to direct Irish influence. Thus the Chester calendar is a record of English activities in Ireland rather than of Irish activities in England.[32]

Another example might be the *Libellus de Ortu Sancti Cuthberti,* a late twelfth-century spurious account of the saint's birth and early life in Ireland, evidently drawn largely from the life of St. Lugaid or Moluag of Lismore. According to Madeleine Hope Dodds, this "little book" may have been commissioned by St. Malachy of Armagh as part of an effort to interest King David I of Scotland and the Cistercian community at Melrose in the small Irish Cistercian community founded by Malachy at the Green Pool in Galloway.

> The point of this particular legend as applied to these particular circumstances is clear. Just as St. Cuthbert came from Ireland to the shores of Scotland, so do these monks come. If the king will befriend them, his country may be honoured by another St. Cuthbert.[33]

The story of St. Cuthbert's Irish origins seems to have been accepted elsewhere, especially at Durham, a noted center of the saint's cult, where the *Libellus* was translated into Middle English about the middle of the fifteenth century, and at York.[34] Both these cathedrals had windows illustrating Cuthbert's Irish birth and early miracles.[35]

Another foundation that may have claimed to possess Irish relics was the secular College of St. Mary in Shrewsbury (or possibly the Lady Chapel of Shrewsbury Abbey), according to O. S. Pickering's recent article, "An Early Middle English Verse Inscription from Shrewsbury," which describes the following entry in Lambeth Palace Library MS 499, a late thirteenth-century Latin manuscript:

> Hec scripta inueniebantur super quoddam vas plumbeum exterius sub fundamento operis capelle beate virginis Salobebire [This inscription was found on a certain leaden vessel under the foundation by laborers at the chapel of the Blessed Virgin in Shrewsbury.]
> Her lis arfaxat fader brandan
> ant kolmkilne ant cowhel þer halewe
> ant dame coroune moder þeyre halewe
>   þat komen in to bretane sautes to seke[36]

These three saints—Brendan, Columkille, and Comhgall—"were apparently known to one another, but were not related, contrary to the statement of the verses,"[37] according to Pickering, and were "famous enough to be known in the West Midlands, but yet sufficiently obscure, in biographical terms, for an assertion of shared parentage to be acceptable."[38] The names "arfaxat" and "coroune" are not attested elsewhere as parents of saints.[39]

The English foundation most famous for its promotion of Irish connections, postconquest, was Glastonbury. It seems likely that Glastonbury did have legitimate ties with Ireland going back at least to the tenth century,[40] and possibly before, but

> [b]y the twelfth century, Glastonbury had begun strenuously asserting the antiquity of its claims to especial sanctity by a variety of means, principal among them the forging of charters. Thus there is one superbly spurious document interpolated into William of Malmesbury's *De Antiquitate Glastoniensis Ecclesiae* which claims to be a letter of St. Patrick describing his arrival at Glastonbury in 430. . . . There are two charters . . . dated 681 . . . and dated 704, in which the Old Church at Glastonbury is described as being dedicated to St. Mary *and St. Patrick.* . . . However, both these are patent forgeries and cannot have been drawn up before the late tenth century at the earliest.[41]

In spite of such questionable methods (which seem to have been viewed as perfectly justified at the time), Glastonbury came to have quite a reputation "for having been a resting place of Irish saints and a haven for wandering Irish monks."[42] William of Malmesbury claimed that Glastonbury held relics of such Irish saints as St. Brigit and St. Benignus, and that St. Patrick and St. Indract were buried on either side of the altar in the church.[43] Michael Lapidge finds evidence that by the early tenth century "Glastonbury was the centre of a cult of St. Patrick and a destination of wandering Irish *peregrini*,"[44] but there is no association of St. Indract with Glastonbury before the second quarter of the eleventh century.[45]

In light of Glastonbury's interest in attracting Irish pilgrims, it seems likely that the monks made an effort to collect Irish manuscripts and to produce their own copies or versions of texts from Irish sources.[46] Some of these may have been used by John of Tynemouth in compiling his monumental fourteenth-century collection, the *Sanctilogium*,[47] reedited in the fifteenth century as *Nova Legenda Anglie*.

Middle English Vernacular Hagiography

We have established that certain Irish saints were known and venerated in medieval England, but most of the evidence so far is found in Latin sources. Which Irish saints were considered popular enough to merit translating their stories into Middle English? The South English Legendary is the earliest and most widespread collection of saints' lives in Middle English. The late thirteenth-century *Early South English Legendary* includes versions of the life of St. Brigit, St. Brendan's voyage, and the tale of St. Patrick's Purgatory and Sir Owain's vision there.[48] The later *South English Legendary* (ca. 1300/1320 for manuscripts used in the D'Evelyn and Mill edition)[49] has a different version of St. Brigit's life which seems much closer to the oldest Irish source, a version of St. Patrick's Purgatory that includes a brief life of St. Patrick himself, a version of St. Brendan's voyage very similar to that in *The Early South English Legendary (ESEL)* (the source for both texts is the *Navigatio Sancti Brendani*),[50] and a life of St. Dunstan which may reflect the association of St. Patrick with Glastonbury.

Of þe hous of Glastyngburi . a gret ordeynor [St. Dunstan] was
And made muche of hore god rule . þat neuere er among hom nas
At þat hous þat was ferst bigonne . four hondred ӡer biuore
And eke þreo & uifti ӡer . ar sein Donston were ibore
For þer was ordres of monkes . ar sein Patrik come
And ar Seint Austin to Engelond . broӡte Cristendom
And seint Patrik deide four hondred . & two & fifti ӡer
After þat oure suete Leuedi . oure Louerd an eorþe ber

(206.45–52)[51]

Charlotte D'Evelyn and Frances A. Foster note, "It is now generally accepted that the *SEL* was intended for the public instruction of the unlettered laity rather than for the use of monks" and that it was probably compiled by friars.[52] The fifty-one extant manuscripts of the *South English Legendary (SEL)* suggest that it was a very popular collection.[53] Thus, the choice of the three aforementioned Irish saints suggests that they were deemed to hold the most interest for English-speaking, lay audiences.

All three of the major stories—St. Brigit, St. Brendan's voyage, and Sir Owain's vision in St. Patrick's Purgatory—probably reflect Anglo-Norman interests, rather than Irish influence. Hennig has argued that the Normans were primarily responsible for promoting devotion to St. Brendan in northwestern Europe from the eleventh century onward,[54] though it was doubtless first introduced by the many Irish exiles and scholars who found their way to France and Germany in the ninth and tenth centuries or perhaps before. St. Brigit, too, had a thriving Continental following long before the Norman Conquest, again probably influenced by Irish scholars in exile (though it may go back even further, to the saint's pagan origins). She is unique, however, in also having a well-established British/English cult, growing from "areas where Irish immigration had . . . taken place in the fifth and sixth centuries A.D.,"[55] all along the west coast of England and throughout Wales and Scotland,[56] so that there must have been a ready audience for her *vita* among the conquered as well as the conquerors. And the tale of Sir Owain is "one of the most widely known mediaeval accounts of the other-world,"[57] and exists in numerous Continental manuscripts. Yet in spite of what we now know about the origins of the stories, contemporary readers must have understood them to contain more or less accurate information. If so, what images of Ireland and the church in Ireland, are conveyed in these saints' lives?

St. Brigit

The appeal of St. Brigit for Middle English audiences may be explained partly by her long-standing cult in Britain and Wales, as stated before. Also, as J. S. P. Tatlock points out in "Greater Irish Saints in Lawman and in England" (in which he argues that Laȝamon was well-acquainted with Ireland and Irish culture), "There was no specially appealing early British woman-saint. Even among miracles in Irish saints' legends, some of hers stand out for imagination, not to say grotesqueness."[58]

The *ESEL* includes a short version (fifty-eight lines) of *Vita sancte Brigide virginis,* which consists of a brisk listing of her major miracles. Most of the distinguishing details have been omitted, and without the introduction ("Seinte Bride of heiȝe men : In scotland heo cam" [1]), it is a story that could have taken place anywhere. The miracles seem brushed over; the emphasis, rather, is on the saint's holiness:

> In lawe of cristindom.
> Þis Maide bi-gan wel ȝong : to beo of porture hende;
> Þare ne scholde vil dede ne word : neuere fram hire wende.
> heo bigan ore louerd crist to serui : in worde and in dede;
> ȝwane hire ȝongue felawes weren atþe pleiȝ : hire oresones heo
>   seide.

(2–6)

With similar hagiographical commonplaces sprinkled throughout the piece, the tone is that of a dull but improving moral tale, ending with, "Þe furste dai of feuerer : hire lijf heo brouȝte to ende . / god us graunti alle forth with hire : [to þe] blisse of heuene wende" (57–58). The miracles attributed to Brigit in this version deal mostly with cows, dairying, shepherding, and housewifely duties such as drying clothes on a sunbeam, and turning water into ale and a stone into salt, but these activities were not unique to Ireland (or "Scotland," which probably did not signify "Ireland" to its late thirteenth- early fourteenth-century audience).[59] However, the fact that these agricultural and housekeeping concerns are uniquely associated with St. Brigit probably accounts, at least in part, for her popularity throughout Europe. Nevertheless, all distinctly Irish features of Brigit's *vita*, such as personal or place names and native customs, are missing from this early, condensed version.

The later *SEL* contains a longer (270 lines) and much more interesting version of Brigit's legend, which clearly reflects its ultimate source (probably the *Third Life*, which was also the source for the life of St. Brigit in John of Tynemouth's early fourteenth-century *Sanctilogium*[60]). It includes a number of details that fall into the pattern, found in some romances, of Ireland as Otherworld island whose residents possess magical powers. The opening and closing of the two versions are similar, but the longer one preserves such distinctive details as the names of Brigit's pagan parents, Duptak and Broksek (3–5); the druids' prophecies of her greatness before she was born (17–42, 55–58); her auspicious birth at dawn on the doorstep ("Noþer wiþinne hous ne wiþoute" [66]—a type of paradoxical formula found frequently in Celtic mythology); her childhood in the household of another druid (Middle English *enchanteor*, 47–110); and her identification with the Virgin Mary (122–40). The recognition of the saint through prophecies and visions of pagan "enchanteors" seems unusual, possibly even unique in European hagiography, though one can imagine how it might have been used as an example of how God reveals himself even to unbelievers.

The druids' prophecies and the unusual circumstances of the saint's conception and birth are typical Irish folklore motifs also found in hero-tales, such as those of Lugh, Finn mac Cumhail, Conchobar, Cú Chulainn, and Conall Cernach. Many Irish saints' conceptions and births followed similar patterns.[61]

> Stories of the coming of saints into the world . . . have a great deal in common with those of the "secular" heroes. Their births are foretold by an angel, another saint, or a druid. . . . St David and St Cynog were the products of rape, St Cadoc's mother was abducted. . . .
>
> St Senán's mother, like the Buddha's, was delivered from the pains of travail, and other miracles are characteristic of the births of saints. The child may speak at birth, or a spring may burst forth and he is baptized in it. . . .
>
> Needless to say, tales of this kind are not peculiar to Celtic mythology. They are the common stuff of birth myths the world over. . . .[62]

Another incident with a distinctive Irish twist to it is that of Brigit's escape from marriage:

Suþþe it biuel þer afterward . þat þis maide ssolde
To a gret duk yspoused be[o] . as al hure vrendes wolde

. . . .
He[o] bad oure louerd niȝt & day . hure wissi and rede
And sende hur þane deþ uppon . þanne do þulke dede
Oþer binime hure on of hure lymes . oþer som lac hure sende
War þoru þe mannes herte . fram hure miȝte wende
Oure Louerd hurde hure bone wel . & hure on eiȝe hure bynom

. . . .
Anon þis ȝonge man þis isey . his herte he gan wiþdrawe
God schulde me he sede . to ssende my sulue so
To wedde a oneyde quene . inelle it neuere do

(221–34)

Brigit then receives her father's permission to become a nun, as he realizes that with only one eye she will never be married, and "So sone so he[o] was nonne imaked . & iconfermed also / Of þe bissop fast inou . þat it nemiȝte noȝt be[o] vndo / Oure Louerd hure sende hure eiȝe aȝen . as god as he was er" (247–49).

Certainly other saints maimed themselves to avoid marriage, but this passage may reflect the ancient Irish law that a ruler (and, by extension, his wife) must be physically unblemished,[63] both in the young duke's refusal—"God shield me from shaming myself so as to wed a one-eyed queen!"—and in God restoring Brigit's eye once she is safely in a nunnery, as if to say that it won't do for a spiritual leader to be physically blemished, either. It is not uncommon for saints to be miraculously healed of mutilations, but St. Brigit's healing may also reflect her native cultural values.

St. Brendan

The *ESEL* version of the voyages of St. Brendan begins with an interesting scribal error. Although the piece is entitled, *"Vita sancti Brendani, Abbatis de Hybernia,"* the first line reads, "Seint bren-dan, þe holi man : was here of ovre londe" (1). I don't see how this can have been a translator's error; *Hybernia* bears no similarity to *terra nostra*. Is it possible that the Middle English translation was made originally in Ireland, which the translator considered "ovre londe"? It seems more likely that a scribe misread a spelling such as "eirlonde" or "yerlonde." There is no further mention of Ireland until the end of the poem:

Seint Brendan, þe holie man : sone to deþe drouȝ—
For neueref[t] aftur þulke tyme : of þe world he ne rouȝte,
Bote as a man of an oþur worlde : and ase he were in þouȝte—
And deide sone in *yrlaunde* : aftur þulke stounde.

(ll. 730–33, italics mine)

If the *SEL* were indeed compiled by friars to be read aloud to laypersons, those listeners could easily have received the impression that St. Brendan was an English saint who happened to die in Ireland. On the other hand, it was a very well-known tale, and perhaps the reader would have translated the Latin title as well. I would not go so far as to say that the *ESEL* shows a deliberate de-Hibernicizing of Sts. Brendan and Brigit, but from "Irlonde" to "ovre londe" seems a bit of a stretch for a scribal error. The next few lines in both versions are almost identical:

Seint brendan, þe holi man : was here of ovre londe.
Monek he was of harde liue : as ich me under-stonde,
Of fastingue and oþur penaunce i-nov : and Abbot he was þere
Of a þousend Monekes : þat alle under him were.

(*ESEL*, ll. 1–4)

Sein Brandan þe holyman . was ȝend of Irlonde
Monk he was of hard lyf . as ich vnderstonde
Of fastynge and penance inou . and abbod he was þere
Of a þousond monkes . þat alle vnder him were.

(*SEL*, ll. 1–4)

And in fact, throughout, both versions are similar enough that they must have the same source.

The story of St. Brendan's voyages was immensely popular in both clerical and lay circles, given the large number of extant manuscripts: a total of 116 in Latin from the tenth to the fifteenth centuries, and numerous vernacular translations from the eleventh century onward, including Anglo-Norman, Old French, Old Provençal, Old Italian, Catalan, Old Dutch, Middle Low German, Middle High German, Middle English, and Norwegian.[64] It had everything—the thrill of discovering the unknown, danger, monsters, death, beauty, and spiritual lessons. Joseph Dunn notes that some Latin sources praise the poem very highly,[65] but not everyone was impressed by the *Navigatio*.

As early as the twelfth century doubts were expressed and protests raised against the Brendan legend. Giraldus Cambrensis had a fling at it when he wrote "these things might truly be thought incredible except that, in those who believe, all things are possible." In the thirteenth century, the learned Dominican, Vincent de Beauvais . . . in his *Speculum Historiale,* was even more severe: "hujus autem peregrinationis historiam," he wrote, "propter apocrypha quaedem deliramenta quae in ea videntur contineri penitus ab opere isto resecamus." . . .

The bitterest attack that was ever launched on the Brendan legend was made by an unknown poet, in a metrical life of St. Brendan in Latin, preserved in an eleventh or twelfth century manuscript at Lincoln College, Oxford. It begins:

> Hic poeta, qui Brendani   uitam uult describere.
> Graue crimen uiro Dei   uidetur inurere.

This poet who would fain write the life of Brendan, seems to attach a serious crime to the man of God.

The author exclaims against the folly of believing that St. Brendan forsook the 3,000 monks who were entrusted to his care and for whose guidance he would have to render an account to God, and that,

> Currens semper ad occasum   uelo, uento, rimige,
> . . . .

Coursing ever towards the west, under sail, with the wind, and by oar, he sought in the sea what is to be found only in heaven.

> O rem miram, risu dignam,   et plenam stulticie!
> Fabulosum est, non uerum,   neque ueri simile.

Oh, how strange, laughable and full of folly—A fable it is, not true nor even truthlike.

He objects to the demons singing praises to the Creator which, he holds, is contrary to Catholic doctrine. Then with a burst of indignation he exclaims:

> O quam macra et infelix   spes est Hibernensium,
> Quibus post hanc vitam   tota merces operum
> Terra nuda et lapilli   atque flores arborum!

How lean and miserable is the hope of the Irish, whose only reward for their labors after this life is a bare land, with stones and the flowers of trees.[66]

Nevertheless, the tale of Brendan's voyages remained popular everywhere, and perhaps what is most significant about the tale is the westward voyage itself. The adventures of the monks, adrift in their coracle and driven by the will of God to all manner of astounding and edifying islands, grew out of the Irish penitential voyages of the sixth to the ninth centuries, as described by James F. Kenney.

> The voyages were made sometimes by single monks, sometimes by small groups. The vessels used were either wooden merchant ships, or, more often, those skin covered coracles which are still found on some parts of the Irish coasts. Occasionally voyages may have been entered on in that fantastic spirit of religious fatalism of which a curious instance is related by the Anglo-Saxon Chronicle as late as 891:

>> Three Irishmen came to King Alfred in a boat without any oars from Ireland; whence they stole away, because they would live in a state of pilgrimage, for the love of God, they recked not where. The boat in which they came was made of two hides and a half; and they took with them provisions for seven nights; and within seven nights they came to land in Cornwall, and soon after went to King Alfred.[67]

Another element was the quest for an earthly Paradise, a land which some Christian writings placed in the extreme east (as does the first part of the Middle English "Voyage": "So þat we dude us in a ssip . and estward euere drowe / in þe se of occean . wiþ tormens inowe" [*SEL* 33–34), but which had also become confused with older traditions of the land of the dead, to be found in the west.[68] Ireland itself came to be regarded with "superstition . . . as being situated in the extreme west, the land of the shades."[69]

When the legend of Brendan's voyage first appears in Middle English in the thirteenth and fourteenth centuries, the idea of Ireland as the jumping-off place of the West was still strong, and continued to have a powerful effect on the English imagination. Kenney noted that this legend, as widespread as it was, influenced the fifteenth-century voyages of discovery that set out for "'the island of Brasylle.'"[70] At least one voyager, in 1480, fully expected to find it "'to the west of Ireland.'"[71]

St. Patrick

Versions of St. Patrick's *vitae* are found in several Middle English sources, the longest in Higden's *Polychronicon,* translated into Middle English by John Trevisa in the fifteenth century. The later *SEL* account of Sir Owain's visit to St. Patrick's Purgatory includes a brief account of the saint's work and more remarkable miracles in Ireland—the driving out of snakes and all poisonous things, the incident of the sheep that baaed from inside the thief who had eaten it, a cross whose power was negated by the burial of a pagan beneath it—leading up to the opening of a gateway to purgatory (as in the earlier version), a description of the religious foundation there, and finally, Sir Owain's journey (ll. 89–716).

The incident of the stolen sheep (ll. 15–24) also appears in the *Alphabet of Tales,* a fifteenth-century Middle English translation of a French Latin text, as a warning against theft.[72] It is certainly both striking and funny, as many of the most effective fables are.

The *SEL* account of how St. Patrick drove all snakes and poisonous things out of Ireland details the remarkable lasting effects:

> Ech treo þat in þe londe grouþ . & eorþe of þe lond also
> Ne þoleþ no venim in none stude . ney him beo ido
> No voul worm necomþ þer ney. þas nis anon lyfles
> Bote a lite ssort euete . and ȝute he is tailles
> Much clannesse & muche god . wo so deþ him vnderstonde
> For þe loue of sein Patrik . oure Louerd dude to al Irlonde
>
> (ll. 9–14)

A similar account may also be found in Giraldus's *Historia et Topographia Hibernia* (1188), but in Middle English, only here and in Trevisa's translation of Higden's *Polychronicon.* Patrick's banishment of snakes from Ireland has become a cliché, but the description of Ireland as a land so pure and healthful that the trees and even the earth will not endure any poison (Giraldus wrote that leaves from Irish plants might be used as an antidote; his source was Bede), and imported snakes die when they near the island (also mentioned by Bede)—such a country, though it might be the result of God's intervention, has something in common with the Otherworld paradise described in earlier Irish writings.

Another brief life of St. Patrick is found in Higden's *Polychronicon,* as translated into Middle English by John Trevisa (V.iv.303–7). Higden's sources were Giraldus Cambrensis and "þe martilogie" (V.305; perhaps the Martyrology of Tallacht?). He distinguishes two St. Patricks, one, "þe firste bisshop of Irlond" (V.303), and "þe lasse Patrik, þat was abbot and nouȝt bisshop, and was in his floures aboute þe ȝere of oure Lord eyȝte hondred and fifty" (V.307). According to the *Polychronicon,* Bishop Patrick was a contemporary of St. Columkille (Columba) and St. Brigit "þat Patrik veillede, and sche overlevede him by sixty ӡere" (V.305). In addition to the banishment of snakes and the foundation of Patrick's Purgatory, Higden attributes a third miracle to St. Patrick (the bishop), "þat he prayed and hadde it i-graunted of God all myӡti, þat non Irische man schal abide þe comynge of Antecrist" (V.305). Higden acknowledges that Patrick's Purgatory is attributed to this first Patrick, but "þat is more acounted to þe lasse Patrick," who "fonde first [in Ireland] a rebel peple, and þerfore he went out of Irlond, and deide in þe abbey of Glastynbury" (V.307). The question of whether there were two (or even three) Patricks is still unresolved, but this theory may have been invented originally to reconcile the existence of St. Patrick's tomb in Ulster (V.305) with the claim that Patrick was buried at Glastonbury (V.307; William of Malmesbury, *De Gestis Regum* 24–25).

The "Irish Life" of St. Cuthbert[73]

The twelfth-century *Libellus de Ortu Sancti Cuthberti,* as mentioned before, is one possible example of hagiography with an ulterior motive—to encourage the King of Scotland to support an Irish monastic community in his territory.[74] The main outline of the story is lifted from the early life of the Irish St. Lugaid or Moluag of Lismore,[75] whose name "Mullok" the writer gives as St. Cuthbert's baptismal name (Middle English *Life* 1.375). This kind of borrowing was evidently quite common in medieval hagiography—even the more creditable *vitae* of St. Cuthbert, by an anonymous monk of Lindisfarne and by Bede, are rife with incidents or passages from other saints' lives.[76] Dodds suggests that a larger purpose of the writer may have been to rehabilitate the Irish saint.

> The Cistercian monks who were Romanizing the Celtic church of Scotland came into conflict with the belief in the earlier Celtic saints. The more thorough-going reformers tried to abolish the old saints altogether. The more thoughtful and sympathetic rewrote the lives of the Celtic saints in order that their flock might still revere them without being injured by any unorthodox teaching.[77]

She goes on to point out the irony that "only a hundred years before, St. Cuthbert had been in exactly the same position with regard to the Benedictines that the Celtic saints were now with the Cistercians."[78] Whatever his intent, the writer "succeeded in turning St. Cuthbert into an Irishman, instead of making St. Lugaid a Benedictine."[79]

The *Libellus,* first compiled in the late twelfth century,[80] seems to have circulated in northern England, as well as in Scotland, and by the fourteenth century had found its way into the traditions of Cuthbert's followers at Durham and York, in particular, two very powerful and influential foundations. John of Tynemouth also included the story in the *Sanctilogium.*[81] The *Libellus* was translated into Middle English verse about the middle of the fifteenth century as part 1 of a four-part account of the saint's life. Part 2 is translated from Bede; part 3 concerns the posthumous miracles of Cuthbert; and part 4,

> a sort of appendix, gives a brief epitome of Cuthbert's life. This is followed by a calculation of his age, and then by an account of the founding of the minsters of Holy Island and Durham and of their later history, from Bede and Symeon. . . .
> By way of conclusion the translator has added an account of the bounds of Islandshire, and of royal and other donations down to 1098, from the *Brevis Relatio.*[82]

The authorities generally agree that part 1, the "Irish Life" of St. Cuthbert is quite without foundation. Even without Dodds's demonstration of the writer's debt to the life of St. Lugaid of Lismore, Charles Eyre noted that "the name *Cuthbert* is undoubtedly Saxon,"[83] and whatever *Cuthbert* means,[84] it is not the Anglo-Saxon equivalent of "Mullocke," as stated in the sixteenth-century *Rites of Durham.*[85] There are numerous anachronistic references— for example, the story that St. Cuthbert (d. 687) and St. Brigit (d. 525) were childhood friends in the household of Columba, bishop of Dunkeld, who cannot really have been St. Columba of Iona (d. 597) (Middle English *Life* ll. 833–90).[86]

On the other hand, we have no other information about the saint's life before age eight, where the earliest (anonymous) account begins. So perhaps, as J. T. Fowler, editor of the Middle English version, suggests, "there may be some germ of historic truth at the bottom of the Irish story."[87] Bertram Colgrave, in the introduction to *Two Lives of St. Cuthbert,* writes, "it is clear that [Cuthbert] belongs to the Celtic rather than to the Roman tradition, and that, in spite of his dying attacks upon the Celtic 'heretics' [*Prose Life* chap. 39], he lived and died after the manner of the typical Irish monk."[88] Throughout these two earliest *vitae* of the saint, Colgrave footnotes a variety of references that might suggest Irish origins or influence, though probably we should attribute them simply to general Celtic influence in Northumbria at the time.

Nevertheless, the "Irish Life" was accepted as legitimate among the faithful of the thirteenth to the fifteenth centuries (and doubtless beyond, in the absence of evidence to the contrary). Once the story was incorporated in John of Tynemouth's extremely popular *Sanctilogium,* it surely became quite well-known, especially since St. Cuthbert was one of the most revered saints in England throughout the medieval period, and had some following in Ireland as well.[89] York and Durham cathedrals, which commemorated Cuthbert's Irish origins in their stained-glass windows, were both popular places of pilgrimage. In addition, the story's romantic characteristics[90] might have made it very popular with lay audiences.

The Middle English version contains numerous references to Irish places and customs and makes use of several motifs from Irish folklore; it thus includes some of the most explicit information about Ireland to be found in Middle English hagiography, even more than the *SEL* life of St. Brigit. Among the identifiable Irish place-names in the "Irish Life" are "lainestyre" (Leinster, l. 71), the realm (or "cite," according to the text) of Cuthbert's maternal grandfather Muriadac, and "connate" (Connaught, l. 74), the neighboring territory of the evil king who murders Muriadac and all his household, except for the princess Sabina, who will be Cuthbert's mother.[91] Cuthbert is baptized "Mullok" at "Hardebrechins" (l. 377), "Ardbraccan, in Meath."[92] The writer cites the testimony of Bishop Eugenius concerning Cuthbert's birthplace.

> In yreland is a grete cite
> Es calde kenanus, as witnes he,
> In prouynce Midia hatt,
> Many men has bene þar att.
> In þat prouynce er pastures gude,
> Cornes, woddis, ryuers and flude;
> Rynnes a ryuer, Mana calde,
> Þurgh' þis cite before talde.
> In þat ilke ryuer
> Er many Fysches of kynes sere.
> In þis cite of kenane
> Þe childe was borne with' in a wane,
> Þe whilk ʒit þe citezenes
> Schewes, as þair story menes;
> And of þe nonnes abbay
> ʒit Standes alde walles, as þai say,
> Þe whilk place, for þe childes memour,
> Es halden ʒit in grete honour,
> And men of þat same lande

> Er ofte for wirschipe þar comande.
> þir thinges redid biscop Eugeny
> Of herdmonens, in þair story

> (ll. 479–500)

Fowler identifies "kenanus" as "Headfort, the old name of Kells in Westmeath" (14), the river "Mana" as "possibly the old word 'Min,' the name of a river in co. Antrim, here some river in Meath" (14); "herdmonens" is Ardmore in Waterford.[93] I do not know whether any tradition of Kells as St. Cuthbert's birthplace ever existed or developed based on this story. Remembering that this was originally the story of St. Lugaid, Dodds suggests that the "alde walles" may have been the ruins of a prehistoric castle or fort at Tailltin [sic], one of the sites for the celebration of Lughnasadh, the festival honoring Lugh, the god of light. One room in the ruins was called "Rath Lughdhach or Lis Lughdhach. . . . Perhaps the church tried to Christianize this heathen place of worship by turning Lug's chamber, possibly his bridal chamber . . . into the birth chamber of St. Lugaid."[94]

The writer identifies some peculiar Irish customs, as well, though not all are necessarily unique to Ireland. For example, he writes:

> It was in yreland a custome,
> Þat ȝong wenchis suld to gyder come,
> In somer tyde, þat seruands ware,
> And samen to þe woddes fare
> To fotte byrdyns of braunches and floures,
> Forto enbelysce þe whenes boures.
> For slyke seruice vnto þe whene
> Of damysels had ay done bene.

> (ll. 165–72)

This "custome" does not seem to be particularly Irish in flavor. Young girls gathering flowers, for a queen's chamber or for the May Queen, is a common enough motif in European folklore,[95] and here it provides a convenient setup for Cuthbert's mother to become separated from the other women, and thus vulnerable to the lustful king's attack.

A more distinctively Irish custom identified by the writer is the mustering of livestock by the bishop, Cuthbert's first foster-father (ll. 385–88). This is the occasion for Cuthbert's first miracle, his prophecy that a black cow will bear a red calf with a white star on its forehead. Cows were fundamental to Irish culture,[96] and Dodds cites numerous incidents involving cows and bulls from saints' lives and other Irish legends.[97] In Irish and Welsh literature, white animals or animals with white markings are often supernatural, coming from the Otherworld.[98]

Also typical is the practice of fosterage, mentioned more specifically in ll. 585–92:

> In yreland was an alde man,
> For halynes grete fame wan,
> he was curtayse and kynde,
> Commyn of noble strynde.
> Gude men sonnes, of þat contre,
> Wer sett to him, norẏst to be;
> He had sex childre ȝeng
> A lang tyme in his kepyng.
>
> (ll. 585–92)

This particular foster-father, however, determines that these boys all have vocations in religion ("he saw þaim loue þe halygaste," l. 593; he saw that they loved the Holy Ghost), and therefore when their families want them to come and take up their worldly inheritances, the old man takes them (along with Cuthbert and his mother) to Britain. This was not the usual practice.

One other custom, which seems unique to this account, is that of wearing a bell, called a "kelym" (l. 426, Irish *ceolan*[99]), around the neck. The boy Cuthbert is given this bell by his father's family as a mark of special favor, "Þe whilk be maner of yreland / About his nek was hyngand" (ll. 427–28). Dodds notes,

> I have not been able to find out anything about the alleged Irish custom of hanging a bell round the neck of a child, but there are endless stories about the sacred bells of the saints of the Celtic church. . . . Reginald of Durham says that in the time of prior Turgot, 1087–1107, there was at Durham a bell of ancient workmanship called a schyll, which was believed to have belonged to St. Cuthbert. It was moderately small, made of an alloy of brass and tin, giving a very sweet sound. It was not a hand bell, but was rung by a cord. It stood on the upper table of the refectory, and in honour of St. Cuthbert, prior Turgot caused it to be ornamented with gold.[100]

Giraldus, writing in the twelfth century, noted that "the people and clergy of both Wales and Ireland have a great reverence for bells that can be carried about" (*History* 116). Cuthbert's bell breaks, and the boy asks a smith to repair it. The smith is willing to do so, but wonders why Cuthbert has brought the bell to him, saying, "Bot to make it I am daft / For I can noȝt of potter craft" (ll. 443–44)—evidently the bell was made of clay. Miraculously, Cuthbert shows the smith how to repair the bell in a furnace fired by rushes.

The role of the smith in this story is perhaps more easily traced. In pagan legends, "smithcraft has a supernatural quality"[101] and a smith is often a magical personage of some kind; Goibniu, one of the godlike Tuatha Dé Danaan, was a smith. In Ireland, metalworking probably retained associations with the Old Religion, and this story may have been meant to illustrate the power of Christ over the pagan gods. The Rees brothers write that "in many parts of the world there is a close connection between iron-working and alchemy and between smiths and initiation into 'men's societies.'"[102] In tales of the youthful exploits of Irish heroes such as Cú Chullain and Finn, a smith sets a test for the boys,[103] but here it is the young St. Cuthbert who tests the smith.

This is but one of the folklore motifs to be found the "Irish Life." Both Dodds and McKeehan have identified many others. I shall mention only those with particularly Irish associations. First, the adulterous or mysterious conception of a special child (ll. 185–96). Cú Chulainn, Cormac Mac Airt, and Mongán Mac Fiachna[104] were among the many heroes of myth and romance whose mothers were ravished by gods or noblemen to be named later.[105] This motif is found in other countries, as well—Greek and Roman mythology, for example—but among saints, the phenomenon seems to be more common in Celtic hagiography; McKeehan cites three Welsh saints and six Irish and Scottish saints so begotten, including St. Brigit, as compared with only one English saint, Edith.[106]

A second Irish motif is the marvelous light that shines around the child so brightly that those who see it from outside suppose at first that the house is on fire (ll. 277–306). Thus is revealed the child's holy destiny. Dodds analyzes this as "one of the stories which shows that St. Lugaid had attracted to himself some of the legends of the Celtic god of light,"[107] but McKeehan notes that this phenomenon is often found in hagiography,[108] especially of Irish saints; she cites SS. Brigit, Columba, Comgall, Mochoemoc, Senan, Samthann, and Tigernac.

The casting adrift of the hero with one or more companions (Middle English Life ll. 743–94) is a very common motif in hagiography and romance.[109] In Celtic hagiography, the Irish St. Kentigern and Scottish St. Blane were also set adrift with their mothers,[110] and according to the Rees brothers, "Other references in Irish texts show that setting adrift was a recognized method of punishment."[111] The stone boat (1. 775), however is peculiarly Irish; McKeehan cites similar incidents in the *vitae* of SS. Kieran, Baldred, Endeus, Mochoemoc, Flannan, Bracan, Lasrian, and Paternus.[112] The writer notes that the Irishmen called the boat a "currok" (Irish *corrach,* coracle[113]).

The story of the Psalter which falls into the sea and is taken by a seal calf, who later returns it unharmed to the saint (ll. 561–76, 731–41), is also reminiscent of incidents in other Irish saints' lives (SS. Kieran and Columcille, e.g.) in which Psalters, Gospels, and other lost possessions are retrieved by animals—seals and fish are common agents.

Finally, there is St. Cuthbert's vision of (or visit to) the land under the sea—as the poem says, "Cuthbert had a vysyoune, / Whether in body or with' oute, / It was to him grete doute" (ll. 632–34). As he and his companions (his mother and the old holy man with his six foster sons) are sailing from Ireland to Britain, Cuthbert dreams that their ship's anchor snags on the roof of a house under the sea. He dives down to free the anchor, and is met by a man who addresses him in Irish and prophesies that Cuthbert will be a "cytesyn of heuen" (1. 658). The sea-man gives Cuthbert three vases, saying that the old holy man will interpret their meaning for him. The sea-man, who is described as "a fair man and auncyene, / And, mewre in face, þat semely sire / Was gliterand as brynnand fire" (ll. 688–90), obviously a divine personage of some kind, then blesses Cuthbert and sends him back up to the ship. The old man tells him that the three vases symbolize the trinity, which Cuthbert shall preach to the heathen; two vases are for the two commandments of love ("Thou shalt love the Lord thy God . . . and thou shalt love thy neighbor as thyself," Matt. 29:19), and the other signifies Cuthbert's future solitary life in religion (ll. 705–16).

According to Dodds, the story of the anchor caught on the house under the sea and the boy who goes down to free it and learns something important from the undersea dwellers probably comes from an early ninth-century legend associated with St. Brigit.[114] In secular Celtic tradition the Otherworld is often portrayed as "the land beneath the wave,"[115] and the divine personage who addresses the boy could also be identified with the sea god Manannán Mac Lir, who prophesied the coming of Christ in the "Voyage of Bran."[116] The three vases, however, seem to be a unique addition of the writer.[117]

The Middle English *Irish Life* ends with the first miracle of the

boy Cuthbert in Lothian: when he was playing with other boys, he
stood on his head, but

> His clathes stode sterk, euen vp ryght,
> And hilde his leggis. . . .
> . . . .
> Þe whilk schewed' takenyng þat he
> Aftir halyman suld be.

(950–56)

This incident is taken from the anonymous Latin life, and provides a smooth transition to the Middle English writer's chapter
2, based on Bede, which begins with Cuthbert's call to a holy life
at age eight. The writer omits the final chapters of the Latin *Libellus,* which deal with the saint's later life and include several
explanations of why women were forbidden to enter Cuthbert's
churches.[118]

We may conclude, then, that the Irish (or pseudo-Irish) saints
whose *vitae* were translated into Middle English and thus joined
the mainstream of influence were those who had some religious or
political connection with England. St. Brigit had numerous English
churches dedicated to her. St. Cuthbert also had a large following,
especially in the north, and his supposed Irish origins may have
helped to support the establishment of an Irish monastic community in Scotland. St. Patrick, through his supposed connections
with Glastonbury, promoted the pilgrim trade to that foundation.
St. Brendan's voyage was simply too good a story to ignore—and
thus, continued the tradition of Ireland as an Otherworldly land of
marvels, a tradition that was further reinforced by the Middle English translations of Irish journeys to Hell and Purgatory.

5

Ireland and the Irish in Visions of the Otherworld and Other Religious and Didactic Writings

Visions of the Otherworld: *St. Patrick's Purgatory* and *Vision of Tundale*

Accounts of visits to the Otherworld are in some ways similar to Voyage accounts, such as St. Brendan's *Navigatio,* but they are either presented as dreams or visions, or, if they are experienced in the flesh, the location is underground, where most medieval people believed Hell to be situated. The dreamer or pilgrim sees (and sometimes experiences) a Purgatorial or even Hellish Otherworld, often going on to glimpse the heavenly realms as well; of the mixture of both pleasant and punishing islands visited by Brendan, only one was specifically represented as the earthly Paradise, and none was actually Heaven, Hell, or Purgatory (although some of the inhabitants, such as Judas, were undergoing purgatorial punishments). Similarly, Irish poets had distinguished two types of adventure tales, the *immram* or voyage on the sea, and the *echtrae,* which usually included a journey into the Otherworld, often underground.[1]

Interest in such tales of the afterlife was high throughout Europe in the twelfth to the fifteenth centuries, and it is worth noting that of the fifteen legends mentioned in the *Manual of Writings in Middle English,* five take place in Ireland or appeared to an Irishman, or both: visits to St. Patrick's Purgatory by Sir Owain (ca. 1179–81 in Latin[2] and late thirteenth-fifteenth century versions in Middle English), by Nicholas (*Legenda aurea,* ca. 1255–66; *Golden Legend,* 1438), and by William Staunton (took place in 1409, two fifteenth-century Middle English manuscripts); the *Vision of Tundale* (midtwelfth century in Latin; late fourteenth/early fifteenth century in Middle English[3]); and the *Vision of Fursey* (Bede, 731;

in the Middle English *Handlyng Synne,* early fourteenth century; *Polychronicon* late fourteenth century; and *An Alphabet of Tales,* fifteenth century[4]).

Regarding the *Vision of Fursey* (a.k.a. Fursa or Furseus), the only complete Middle English version is found in the fourteenth- and fifteenth-century translations of Higden's *Polychronicon,* which begin by stating clearly that "an holy man þat hiȝte Furseus com out of Irlond into þe province of Est Angles" (VI.9 [Trevisa]) and "a holy man, Furseus by name, come from Yrlonde to the este province of Englische men" (VI.9 [Manuscript Harl. 2261]); Higden's source was Bede. As just noted, St. Fursey was venerated at Canterbury as an Irish saint, and is included in a number of liturgical calendars and Latin collections of *vitae,* such as the *Acta Sanctorum.* However, all references to the saint's Irish origins[5] have vanished from other Middle English references to his vision, both of which emphasize the evils of usury by focusing on one episode of the vision in which Fursa is burned by one of the damned souls because he is wearing a cloak which was given him by a usurer (*Handlyng Synne* ll. 2523–64; *Alphabet* 208). Thomas Wright also notes a late twelfth- or early thirteenth-century French account of the vision "worked up and told again of a monk of Canterbury, which seems to show that the original story was not then so popular as it had been."[6]

The legend of Sir Owain's visit to St. Patrick's Purgatory and the *Vision of Tundale* were the most popular of these legends. Sir Owain visited Lough Derg, the site of St. Patrick's Purgatory, sometime about the middle of the twelfth century. The usual date given is 1153,[7] but Robert Easting has marshaled a variety of evidence for an earlier date, "(no later than) c. 1146–47."[8] Owain's story was later recorded by a Benedictine monk, Henry of Saltrey. According to Wright, "There can be no doubt that by this story St. Patrick's Purgatory was first made known to the world; but it seems very probable that the place had already been occupied by the monks, and that in Ireland it was regarded with superstitious awe."[9] The earliest reference to pilgrimage to the Purgatory is about 1152, when Devorgilla, wife of Tiernan O'Rourke, "sent a message to Dermot MacMurrough asking him to come and take her away, as her husband . . . was absent on a pilgrimage 'to the cave of St. Patrick's Purgatory.'"[10] Her elopement with MacMurrough would set off the events which led to the Norman Conquest of Ireland.

The tale of Sir Owain's experiences spread throughout Europe, and was translated into several vernaculars, including at least three

French metrical versions, one by Marie de France. Surely part of its appeal was the idea of an actual, physical location that gave the faithful access to the Otherworld, as was a similar promise, offered by St. Brendan's voyage, of discovering an earthly Paradise. Wright notes:

> It is clear from the allusion to it in Cæsarius of Heisterbach, that already at the beginning of the thirteenth century, St. Patrick's purgatory had become famous throughout Europe. "If anyone doubt of purgatory," says this writer, "let him go to Scotland [i.e. Ireland, to which this name was anciently given] and enter the purgatory of St. Patrick, and his doubts will be expelled." This recommendation was frequently acted upon in that, and particularly in the following century, when pilgrims from all parts of Europe, some of them men of rank and wealth, repaired to this abode of superstition. On the patent roles in the Tower of London, under the year 1358, we have an instance of testimonials given by the king (Edward III) on the same day, to two distinguished foreigners, one a noble Hungarian, the other a Lombard, Nicholas de Beccariis, of their having faithfully performed this pilgrimage.[11]

The *Manual of Writings in Middle English* lists the following Middle English manuscripts:

> [T]he *South English Legendary* has Owayn's visit in ten manuscripts (varying in length up to 712 verses); and five other versions are known: a stanzaic version of 198 stanzas, incomplete, in the Auchinleck Manuscript; an early couplet version (342 short couplets, fifteenth century); a later couplet version (341 similar couplets); the Harley fragment, two folios of fifteenth century quatrains, based on the *South English Legendary;* and the Hearne fragment, nine quatrains from his edition of the *Scoti-Chronicon.*[12]

Further evidence of the story's popularity is the probability that Chaucer drew on the *ESEL* version for the friar's description of purgatory in the *Sumner's Tale.* As Mabel A. Stanford pointed out, "It is not quite necessary to suppose that he reflects some single account; but if he does, none was so well known, none is so much like the friar's account, as *Saint Patrick's Purgatory.*"[13]

The *ESEL* includes an account of the Purgatory, 673 lines, with no mention of St. Patrick himself beyond the details of the discovery or opening of the pit:

> Seint paterik þoru godes grace: makede ane put in Irlonde,
> Þat seint patrike purgatorie is icleoped : ȝeot, ase ich onderstonde.

Ore louerd him bi-tok ane staf : mid is owene honde,
Þat he fond þulke purgatorie with : i-hered beo godes sonde!
In Irlonde is ӡeot þilke staf i-wust : dereworþeliche i-novӡ,
For gret relike he is i-holde : and elles it were wouӡ.
Seint paterik in þulke stude : þat his purgatorie is,
Of religion bi-gan an hous : þat ӡeot stant, i-wis,
Ant Chanoynes þare-inne he makede : ase ӡeot þare beoth al-so.

                                                        (1–9)

The purgatory experienced by Sir Owain owes its details (directly or indirectly) to a variety of other works concerning the afterlife, especially the *Visio Sancti Pauli*,[14] and possibly the *Vision of Tundale*,[15] an earlier Irish work, which also enjoyed widespread popularity. St. John D. Seymour emphasizes that "the account of the vision was narrated by one Englishman, and written down in England by another, who certainly drew on non-Irish literary sources."[16] Thus, aside from the facts that Owain was an Irish knight who served under an Irish king,[17] and that the Purgatory cave is in Ireland,

> in [the story's] literary form and matter there is nothing that can be described as distinctively Irish in it. . . . It is probable that it represents the eschatological views held in Ireland at the close of the twelfth century, but such would in no way differ from those to be found in England at the same period.[18]

And it must be noted that a later stanzaic Middle English version, the early fourteenth-century, *Owayne Miles,*

> suggests that Owein [*sic*] was born in Northumberland. . . . The English versifier, providing a poem for a secular English audience, aimed for immediacy by making his knightly hero "one of us," and possibly had in mind the most famous Northumbrian to have a vision of the otherworld, Bede's Drihthelm.[19]

The tale of St. Patrick's Purgatory, then, is one that attracted a great deal of attention to Ireland, without telling its readers very much about Ireland itself, except to add to the haze of mystery already clouding that island. The two Middle English prose accounts add nothing further to the legend. In the early fifteenth-century vision of William Staunton, St. Patrick's Purgatory becomes a framework for a complaint against the vices of Staunton's time, especially "extravagant fashions in dress"[20] and the "failings of the clergy."[21] Staunton's guides are two very English saints, St.

John of Bridlington and St. Ive. The journey of Nicholas, found in the 1438 *Golden Legend,* "is similar to Owayn's [*sic*], but much shorter."[22]

The *Vision of Tundale,* however, retains several distinctly Irish references even in its Middle English versions, though one of the most interesting, again, was lost in translation (with one manuscript exception; see the following section). The original Latin *Visio Tnugdali* was written by an Irish monk, Marcus, in Regensburg, Southern Germany, in the midtwelfth century, and became extremely popular.[23] According to the latest editor of the Middle English version, Rodney Mearns, "Recent surveys have identified 184 MSS of the tale, 149 of which are in Latin. Printed texts of 15 medieval vernacular translations are known, not counting instances where more than one translation was made into the same language."[24] The English translation "survives in whole or in part in five mid- or late-fifteenth-century MSS,"[25] and is based on the version found in Vincent of Beauvais's *Speculum Historialis* (1244–54), a work which was well-known throughout Europe.[26] Vincent, in turn, had copied the story from a Cistercian chronicler, Helinand of Froidmont, who had condensed Marcus's original by omitting the prologue and a section describing the topography of Ireland.[27] Thus we will never know whether Middle English writers would have found this description worth including or not. However, the writer of one manuscript (A), Richard Heeg, seems to have had Marcus's Latin text available to him as well as a Middle English text based on Vincent, and thus adds or modifies a number of passages,[28] but does not include the topography of Ireland. The most telling addition follows the description of two giants Tundale sees being tortured:

> Off whom þo names were called þus,
> þat ton hyȝt Forcusuo & þat toder Conallus.
> "Alas," quod þat sowle, "suche peyn haue þey
> Wheder þei schull neuer þennes away."
> Quod þe angell, þe falon no glee;
> "And in erþe seche hast þou ybe."
>
> (MS A, ll. 551–56)

Notes Mearns, "The two names, Fergusius and Conallus feature in Marcus, but are omitted by Helinand and so by Vincent. . . . The names, which refer to characters in native Irish mythology, could not have been available to him in any other way [except from Marcus's version], and they occur at the same place in his narrative as in the original."[29] For this study, this is one of the most interesting passages in the poem, since it is one of the very few references in Middle English literature to recognizable characters from Irish mythology—Fergus Mac Roich and Conall Cernach of the *Táin Bó Cuailgne*. Unfortunately, I cannot attach as much significance to it as I would wish, because Manuscript A, according to Mearns, is not a source for any of the other Middle English texts, and in fact

> is later than the others by possibly as much as three decades. Furthermore, as is the case with the other works in this MS, it is this version above all which is wayward and constantly idiosyncratic and has most clearly suffered scribal interference. . . . [F]ar from being closest to the archetype, A, the fullest copy of the poem to have come down to us, is the furthest removed from the author's original. . . .[30]

The more reliable Middle English manuscripts, however, do retain a number of other Irish features from the Latin original. The question remains, of course: To what extent would they have been recognized as such by middle English readers? As Mearns points out, the Middle English version "is markedly popular in character, and was written neither for a genteel audience nor for a scholarly one."[31]

The poem does state clearly at the beginning that Tundale was an Irishman:

> In Yrlonde byfell somtyme þys case
>
> . . . .
> I woll ȝou telle how hyt befell þanne
> In Yrlonde of a ryche manne;
> Tundale was hys ryȝth name,
> He was a mon of wykked fame.
> He hadde ynowȝ of all rychesse,
> But he was pore of all godenesse
>
> (11, 17–22)

The poem details Tundale's sins of commission (treachery, pride, anger, envy, lechery, gluttony, covetousness, and sloth) and omission (no merciful deeds, not loving God or church, no charity or pity). In addition, Tundale encourages jugglers, lecherers, and other "mysdoeres," and all kinds of strife (23–35). In short, "Ther was no man lyued worse lyfe" (36). The concept of the "wild Irish" was well entrenched by the time of these Middle English texts, and a wicked man like Tundale fit the stereotype better than the admirable Fursey or Owain (in *Owayne Miles*). Tundale is converted through his vision, however, and wakes up a reformed character (121–38)—very encouraging both from a spiritual and (perhaps) cultural point of view.

Another incident in the poem, with a typically Irish twist which might have amused English readers, is Tundale's encounter with a narrow bridge (a common motif in Otherworld journeys) over a lake full of monsters:

> Two myle hyt was on lengthe semande
> and skarslye þe brede of an hande;
> Wyth sharpe pyles of iren & stele
> Hyt was þykkesette, & greuows to fele.
>
> (607–10)

Tundale must not only cross this bridge, but also lead across with him a wild cow as a punishment for stealing a cow from his godfather. Cattle raiding had been a time-honored tradition among the Irish since the iron age,[32] and likely was still common in the fourteenth and fifteenth centuries. No doubt the Irish found rustling the English colonists' cattle even more rewarding than raiding each other's. The lines that follow present a striking mixture of the ridiculous and the terrifying:

> Mawgray hys hede he moste nede
> Take þe kowe & forth her lede.
> .   .   .   .
> The kowe by þe horne he hente.
> He cheryste þe kowe all þat he myȝte,
> To þe brygge he ladde her ryȝte;
> When he on þe brygge was
> The kowe wolde no forþer passe.
> He saw þe beestes of þe lake
> Drewe ner þe brygge her pray to take.
> The kowe fyll downe þat tyde
> And Tundale at þat oþer syde.
> Tundale was full ferde þanne,
> Wyth grete drede vp a aȝeyn he wanne.
>
> (681–96)

In the middle of the bridge, Tundale and the cow encounter another thief who carries a sheaf of wheat. Neither will give way, nor can they pass one another, so they stand there weeping with frustration until the angel takes pity on Tundale and "browte him fro þat woo, / And badde hym late þe kowe goo" (719–20).

After Tundale and his angelic guide enter the outskirts of heaven,[33] he encounters three contemporary Irish kings whom he had known when they were alive. First, the two rivals "Concelere" and "Donate" (Conor O'Brien and Donagh MacCarthy[34]). In life, Tundale remembers, "In hem was lytull mercy sene; / Eyþer of hem hatede oþer / As cursede Kaym dyde hys broþer" (1610–12), so he is surprised to find them here. The angel tells him that the two kings had repented later and done penance, so that God had forgiven them (1617–38).

Further on, Tundale and the angel enter a gorgeous hall where they find King Cormac MacCarthy,[35] who in life had been Tundale's own lord. The King is attended by numerous priests, deacons, and other people who present him with rich treasures of all kinds. Tundale is surprised that he does not recognize any of Cormac's household among them, but the angel says:

> Tho þat þou doste her sye
> Wer non of hys owne maynye,
> But pore pylgrymes þey wer kydde
> To whom he often almesse dyde.
>
> (1705–8)

Cormac's afterlife is not all bliss, however, for he has not yet been forgiven for two mortal sins, adultery and murder. Therefore, for three hours a day, he must leave his beautiful hall and stand in a pit of fire up to his waist (for adultery), wearing a hair shirt (for murder). The poem specifies that Cormac "commandede for to slo / An erle þat he hatede as hys foo, / . . . / Faste by Saynte Patrykes stede" (1741–44)—suggesting that both these sins of Cormac were well-known by the original author, Marcus, and his contemporary audience.[36] What a fifteenth-century Middle English audience thought of it is hard to say. The Irish by this time did have a reputation for treachery (Robert of Gloucester II.10, 782–809; Capgrave's *Abbreuiacion of Cronicles* 210; Giraldus Cambrensis, et al.), and Cormac's sins fit that stereotype neatly.

Tundale and his guide finally reach Heaven itself, where he is met by "Rowdanne," St. Ruadan, his patron saint.[37] Then they are approached by a congregation of bishops, led by St. Patrick. Among them Tundale recognizes Celsus ("Celestyn" [2195]), Malachy of Armagh (2199), "Crystyne" (2212), brother of Malachy and bishop of Clogher,[38] and Neomye (2220), bishop of Cloyne,[39] all leaders in the twelfth-century reform movement, who died not long before the vision took place. Near the four bishops Tundale sees an empty seat, which St. Malachy tells him is reserved "for on of owre brederen dere / that comes not ȝette . . ." (2233–34). "Friedel & Meyer (1907:viii) suggested that this was a polite reference to Bernard [of Clairvaux, d. 1153]," but Spilling argued that it was just as likely to be "somebody in the native Church, Malachy's or Neomye's successor."[40] Such a reference would have been clearly understood by the poem's original audience, particularly by the Benedictine abbess Gisel of *Weihsankpaul,* to whom Marcus dedicated the *Visio.*[41] Once again, however, it would have been lost on a nonscholarly Middle-English audience. If they assigned the empty chair to anyone, St. Bernard would probably have been the more likely candidate.

Mirk's *Festial, Handlyng Synne,* and *The Dicts and Sayings of the Philosophers*

One might have expected to find Irishmen, especially Irish clerics, to figure prominently in the *exempla* of thirteenth–fifteenth century sermons and other didactic writings, considering the lengths to which the English church had gone to reform the Irish church. Indeed, numerous references to Irish clerics and laypersons are found in the Franciscan *Liber Exemplorum,* a Latin text of Anglo-Irish provenance. Giraldus Cambrensis's description of the disappearing islands off the Irish coast *(Topographia)* is used in Latin sermons by the English Bishop Brunton of Rochester and the Austin friar John Waldeby,[42] reflecting the fact that "many men have great liking to hear of strange things of diverse countries," as Sir John Mandeville noted.[43] And a certain treatise called *Quoniam* includes the following reference in its discussion of lecherous clerics:

> Sed certe non est mirum si multi sacerdotum sint luxuriosi, quia nunquam legerunt nisi usque ad Ouvidium / *De arte amandi,* et tunc ordinati in Hybernia resumpserunt lecciones amoris ubi dimiserunt. Aggei 2.d: "Interroga sacerdotes. . . ." [Haggai 2:12–13] (Durham, Cathedral MS B.I.18, fol. 126v, a–b; also in Dublin, Trinity College MS 306, vol. 111v)

Prof. Seigfried Wenzel, who kindly brought this passage to my attention, reads it as "indirectly [criticizing] priests for being ordained, especially in Ireland, before finishing a complete university education."[44] In Middle English sermons from England, however,

I have only found a few references, all in John Mirk's *Festial,* a collection of sermons for every occasion,[45] and in the *Alphabet of Tales,* as just mentioned, an excerpt from the *Vision of Fursa* which does not mention Fursa's nationality, and an incident from the *Life* of St. Patrick.

Similarly, in didactic writings, an Anglo-Irish version of *The Gouvernance of Princes,* by James Yonge, dedicated to the Earl of Ormond, includes frequent illustrations of the book's principles taken from historical events in Ireland, especially those in which the Earl's family had been involved.[46] In English didactic works, however, I have only found one example in one version *The Dicts and Sayings of the Philosophers* (midfifteenth century),[47] and an excerpt from the *Vision of Fursa* in Robert Mannyng of Brunne's *Handlyng Synne,* essentially the same as that found in the *Alphabet of Tales.*

John Mirk, a canon in the Augustinian abbey of Lilleshall in Shropshire, compiled the *Festial* to be used by clerics who were handicapped by "defaute of bokus and sympulnys of letture" ("Prologue").[48] It became "the most widely read vernacular sermon cycle of the fifteenth century, to judge both by the quantity of its surviving manuscripts and by the editions printed by Caxton from 1483 onwards."[49] The date of the *Festial* has usually been given as ca. 1420, but recently Susan Powell has published convincing evidence for an earlier date, between 1350 and 1390.[50]

Of Mirk's two references to Irishmen, the first example warns that good deeds performed only to enhance one's own reputation are worthless in the sight of God.

> I rede þat þer was a wondyr rych man, som tyme, yn Eirlond, and dyd so mony almys-dedys yn hys lyue, þat all men wendon þat he had been a gret seynt before God. But when he was ded, he apered to won þat loued hym wele yn his lyue, as blak as pyche wyth an horrybull stenche, and sayde to hym: "ȝe wenyn I am a saynt; but now I am such as þou may see." Then sayde þat oþer: "Wher byn all þyn almys-deden bycomen?" Þen sayde he: "Þe wynd of vayn glorye hathe blowen hom away." Thus he þat doth almys-dedys for vayne glorie, he leseth all his mede, and fendys of þe ayre strien hit (71).

The main character in this cautionary tale is a rich layman, and it is difficult to find any significance in his being "yn Eirlond," beyond the additional versimilitude provided by a specific setting. Several other narratives in the *Festial* specify real places such as Crowland (a town in Lincolnshire, 239), Rome (17), and Wiltshire (242). The other major example that refers to Ireland in the *Festial* warns priests (and laypersons, as well) against foolish, or suggestive talk.

> For rybawdy and vice ys poyson to a prystys mowth and atture, for hit poysynnyth his one sowle, and envenomyth oþir þat heryn hym. . . .
> I rede þat þer was a prest in Yerlond þat was lusty to speke of rybawdy and iapys þat turnyd men to lechery. Þe whech, yn a nyȝt, wyth fendys was fachyd out of his bed, and soo was out thre days and þre nyȝtys. But yn þe thryd nyȝt he was broght agayne to his bed all forbeten and brent, and al his body ful of choynus as a erthyn woch aȝeynys þe sonne. Þe whech choynus stonk as a pulled honde euermor aftyr whil he lyfuyd and myght neuer aftyr be hole, by no craft. And þen he told how þat fendys brendon hym and beton hym so, so he was lusty for to defowle his mowth wyth fylþ of ribawdy. And al his lyf aftyr, when he herd any mon speke of rybaudy, he wold say a, "Syr, be war be me" (192)

Since Mirk includes examples of sinful priests and nuns in several other sermons, and only one is identified as Irish, I would not say that Mirk views Irish clerics as any worse than English or French clerics.[51] I have not been able to determine the specific source of either of these narratives; however, it seems that Mirk drew much of his material from Jacobus de Voragine's *Legenda Aurea*.[52]

The only other references to Irish priests I found in Middle English were in the long debate poem *The Owl and the Nightingale* (early fourteenth century) and in *Piers Plowman* (B-text, midfourteenth century).[53] The Owl says to the Nightingale, "Þu chaterest so doth on irish prost" (l. 322). No one seems to know exactly what this means, but it is certainly meant to be insulting. Perhaps it refers to the Irish priests' accent or their way of saying the Mass. Stanley suggests, "Perhaps because Irish priests jabber in Irish."[54] Or it could reflect a stereotype of Irish clerics as overtalkative, prone to vain gossip, "rybawdy and iapys" (Mirk 192), which would fit the Owl's general opinion of the Nightingale. The comparison need not imply that the author of the poem had ever been to Ireland, as it is just as likely that he would encounter Irish clergymen in England or elsewhere. As Kathryn Huganir put it, "Irish priests were always abroad."[55] Even though the Nightingale "chatters like an Irish priest," the Owl later points out that she never sings in Ireland, where people need to hear her cheerful sounds:

> Wi nultu singe an oder þeode
> Þar hit is muchele more neode?
> Þu neauer ne singst in Irlonde,

Ne þu ne cumest noȝt in Scotlonde.
Hwi nultu fare to Noreweie,
An singin men of Galeweie,
Þar beoþ men þat lutle kunne
Of songe þat is bineoðe þe sunne?

(ll. 905–12)[56]

The more detailed reference to Irish priests in *Piers Plowman*
runs as follows:

"By þe Marie!" quod a mansed preest, was of þe March of Irlonde,
"I counte na moore Conscience by so I cacche siluer
Than I do to drynke a drauȝte of good ale."
And so seiden sixty of þe same contree,
And shotten ayein wiþ shot, many a sheef of oþes,
And brode hoked arwes, goddes herte and hise nayles,
And hadden almoost vnitee and holynesse adown.
Conscience cryede, "help, Clergie or I falle
Thoruȝ inparfite preestes and prelates of holy chirche."

(XX.221–29)

This is the one reference to Ireland and the Irish in the works
of Langland, the other literary giant of the Middle English period.[57]
In an allegorical poem such as *Piers Plowman,* however, it carries
more weight than would a mere anecdote in another context. Also,
the passage mentions not just one Irish priest, but one supported
by "sixty of þe same contree" (224), which suggests the existence
of a stereotype of Irish clerics as corrupt, drunken, and profane;
again, compare the *exemplum* from Mirk's *Festial* concerning "a
prest in Yerlond þat was lusty to speke of rybawdy and iapys þat
turnyd men to lechery" (192) and the passage in Higden's *Polychronicon* that refers to drunken priests.

Clerkes of þis lond beeþ chast, and biddeþ meny bedes, and dooþ
greet abstinence a day, and drynkeþ al nyȝt; so þat it is accounted for
a myracle þat leccherie reigneþ nouȝt þere, as wyn reigneþ. (I.377–79)

Mirk also cites two incidents from the *Navigatio Sancti Brendani.* The first is Brendan's encounter with Judas Iscariot, who is
allowed to spend certain holy days on an island in the sea, rather
than in Hell, because God is merciful (80). After this digression on
God's mercy, Mirk returns to the focus of the sermon, St. Matthias,
the apostle chosen by lot as Judas's replacement. The second example from the *Navigatio* is found in the sermon for the feast of

St. Michael the archangel, and tells how St. Brendan found on an island a tree full of white birds who had been neutral angels in the battle between St. Michael and Lucifer; for their ambivalence, they also were driven out of Heaven, but they still worship God and "haue non oþir payne, but only þat we ben put out of Godys presence" (260).

Turning to *The Dicts and Sayings of the Philosophers,* a fifteenth-century collection of proverbs and moral tales, we find one reference to Ireland in one manuscript of this very popular work. *The Dicts and Sayings of the Philosophers* was translated into English from the French *Dits Moraulx* of Guillaume de Tignonville, the origins of which go back to an eleventh-century Arabic text.[58] The manuscript, Lord Tollemache's Manuscript, Helmingham Hall (HH), is dated by Bühler ca. 1460, and is a transcription of an unique anonymous translation from the French, which Bühler describes as "unquestionably more complete and more accurate than either the Scrope or the Rivers translation," those being the sources of the other twelve extant manuscripts.[59]

In this one manuscript, then, we find one reference to Ireland in the following brief exchange:

> and anothir seide to a man of Irelonde, by weye of manace: I wole do peyne for to destroye the; to whome the thothir aunsuerd: and I wold do my peyne to appese thyne ire. (265)

The same passage in the Scrope translation is essentially the same, except for the introductory phrase, which reads, "And a-nother callid Hukale said bi way of manace . . ." (264), not specifying to whom the threat is addressed. Whether or not the Helmingham Hall manuscript version is correctly translated, this is an exceptional portrayal of an Irishman as giving a "soft answer" that "turns away wrath."[60] However, since it is a unique manuscript of a unique translation of the text, it probably was not well-known.

The Life of Edward the Confessor and The Book of Margery Kempe

Crippled Irishmen appear in both the *Life of Edward the Confessor* and in *The Book of Margery Kempe.*[61] This is the only similarity between these two works composed at nearly opposite ends of the Middle English period, and can hardly be supposed to indicate anything significant about the reputation of Irishmen in general.

However, a possible parallel is found in Giraldus Cambrensis's late twelfth-century *Historia et Topographia Hibernica.*

> I have never seen among any other people so many blind by birth, so many lame, so many maimed in body, and so many suffering from some natural defect. Just as those that are well-formed are magnificent and second to none, so those that are badly formed have not their like elsewhere. And just as those who are kindly fashioned by nature turn out fine, so those that are without nature's blessing turn out in a horrible way.
>
> And it is not surprising if nature sometimes produces such beings contrary to her ordinary laws when dealing with a people that is adulterous, incestuous, unlawfully conceived and born, outside the law, and shamefully abusing nature herself in spiteful and horrible practices. It seems a just punishment from God that those who do not look to him with the interior light of the mind, should often grieve in being deprived of the gift of light that is bodily and external. (*History* 117–18)

This passage was later paraphrased by Higden in the *Polychronicon* (midfourteenth century), which was then translated into Middle English by John Trevisa (1387).

> Þere beeþ meny men in þis lond wonder foule and yuel i-schape yn lymes and in body. For in hir lymes lakkeþ þe benefice of kynde, so þat nowher beeþ no better i-schape, þan þey þat beeþ þere wel i-schape; and nowher non worse i-schape þan þey þat beeþ þere euel i-schape. And skilfulliche kynde, i-hurt and defouled by wykkednesse of lyuynge, bryngeþ forþ suche foule gromes and euel i-schape of hem þat wiþ vnlaweful weddynge wiþ foule maneres and euel lyuynge so wikedliche defouleþ kynde. (I. 359).

The life of Edward the Confessor was translated into Middle English from a French translation of his Latin *vita* by Ailred of Rievaulx,[62] first into prose, in the late twelfth century, and later into verse, probably in the time of Edward I (1272–1307).[63] The *Book of Margery Kempe* (ca. 1450) is considered the first autobiography in English, though it deals mostly with Margery's pilgrimages and her search for spiritual understanding,[64] and was dictated by Margery herself after she had ceased her travels.

The miracle of the healing of the Irish cripple, Gilemichel, is found in every version of the Life of Edward the Confessor. The story goes that once when King Edward was at Westminster (which he founded), this Gilemichel came to the King seeking healing:

> his senwes were forschronke
> at his bottokkis his helen were his lymes roteþe & stonke

¶op tuei crocches he crep as hit lutle trestles were
so grislich his was to biholde þet hit was gret fere
("Verse Life" ll. 533–36)[65]

Gilemichel begs the King's chamberlain to take him to the King. He has been to Rome six times, and was told by St. Peter in a vision that he would be healed if King Edward carried him to the new church. The King doesn't hesitate to do so, in spite of the cripple's dirty clothes and rotting flesh. The courtiers say the King is mad or bewitched and urge him to drop Gilemichel at the church door where the cure begins to take effect, but the King carries him on into the church. By the time they reach the altar, Gilemichel's legs are normal and he is completely restored. He leaves his crutches at the church and goes back to Rome to thank St. Peter. King Edward founds an abbey dedicated to St. Peter.

Pilgrimages to Rome and elsewhere in search of healing are typical of the period, and not restricted to the Irish. Two details in the prose *Life* (originally translated in the late twelfth century) may indicate a more negative view of the Irish that could reflect the actively anti-Irish attitudes of Giraldus and others of the same period. The fifteenth-century manuscript of the prose version (Manuscript Trinity College Oxford XI) says, "Gyles Michel . . . had a wylde crope" (117), which might be interpreted as describing a outlandishly short haircut. Whether this would be understood as typically Irish or not is questionable; untrimmed beards are more common features for Irishmen. However, the phrase is probably a scribal error, for the corresponding passage in the verse *Life* reads, "A crepel com out of yrlond þet *icrope hadde wel wide*" (l. 532, italics mine). Not having access to the French version, I cannot be certain.

Perhaps a more significant translation in the prose *Life* is Gilemichel's appeal to Hugelyn, the King's chamberlain. "Hugelyn, quoþ he haue reuthe on me þat am þus mys-bred & borne" (117), which I read as meaning that Gilemichel's deformity was congenital. The later verse *Life* reads, "haue reuþe of me þet þus am forbreide" (l. 538), that is, simply, "deformed," without any of the negative connotations attached in medieval times to birth defects, which were often considered punishment for sins—as amply attested by the previous passage from Giraldus.[66]

Turning to the crippled Irishman in *The Book of Margery Kempe,* we find Margery on her way to Rome, abandoned by her traveling companions in Venice, and at a loss for how to get to Rome or back to England without a guide.

Than a-non, as sche lokyd on þe on syde, sche say a powyr man sittyng whech had a gret cowche on his bakke. His cloþis were al for-clowtyd, & he semyd a man of L wyntyr age. Þan sche went to hym & seyde, "Gode man, what eyleth ȝowr bak?" He sayd, "Damsel, it was brokyn in a sekenes." Sche askyd what was hys name & what cuntreman he was. He seyd hys name was Richard & he was of Erlond. (76)

Margery recalls a prophecy given to her by an anchorite in England that a broken-backed man would help her on her travels. She convinces Richard that if he helps her, God will keep them both safe. Soon thereafter, they meet two Grey Friars and another woman on their way to England, and Richard tells Margery:

Þu xalt go forth wyth þes too men & woman, & I xal metyn wyth þe at morwyn & at euyn, for I must gon on my purchase & beggyn my leuyng. & so sche ded aftry his cownsel & went forth wyth þe frerys & þe woman. 7 non of hem cowde vndirstand hir langage, & ȝet þei ordeyned for hir euery day mete, drynke, & herborwe as wel as he dedyn for hem-selfe & raþar bettyr þat sche was euyr bownden to prey for hem. & euery euyn & morwyn Richard wyth þe broke bak cam & comfortyd hir as he had promysed. . . . (76–77, 80, 92)

Louise Collis, in her retelling of Margery's book, *Memoirs of a Medieval Woman,* gives this commentary on Richard:

One can only speculate as to what sort of Irishman Richard can have been. A true native of that island in the fifteenth century would have had a Gaelic name and spoken the Irish language. He may have been a Celt from the country round Dublin who had learned English and taken an English name. Or, he may simply have been an Englishman resident in those parts. As to why he should have been reduced to beggary in Venice, again one can merely offer possible explanations. From Margery's later adventures, it appears that he was gradually making his way back to Ireland. Perhaps, therefore, he was a pilgrim who had met with misfortune. He refers obscurely to "myn enmys" at a certain point in his bargaining with Margery. Whatever his origins, he proved a faithful servant. Neither God, the holy anchorite, nor Margery, had been deceived in their choice of escort.[67]

The suggestion that Richard was or had been a pilgrim, seems quite plausible. He may well have been seeking healing in Rome. I suspect that begging was, or had become, his profession, since his handicap both prevented him from doing physical labor and provided the kind of deformity so useful in arousing the pity of passersby.

Margery seems to have had little or no money herself at this time, as she had to depend on her companions for food and shelter. She also borrowed money from Richard in Rome, and then, "be þe byddyng of God sche ȝaf a-wey to powr pepil al þe mony þat sche had, & þat sche had borwyd of hym also (106). Richard was understandably angry about this prodigality, which Margery felt was justified "by þe byddyng of God." She promised to pay him after she returned to England, setting a rendezvous at Bristol. Two years later, she went to meet him there.

> And owr Lord Ihesu Crist had so ordeyned for hir, as sche went to-Bristowe-ward, þat þer was ȝouyn hir so meche mony þat sche myth wel payn þe forseyd man al þat sche awt him. & so sche dede, blissed by owr Lord þerfor. (108)

Margery Kempe, who was illiterate, could scarcely have been aware of Giraldus's scathing account of Irish deformities, nor of Higden's version. The prophecy that leads her to Richard did not specify that he would be Irish. And in most ways, Richard is not a stereotypical Irishman, except perhaps in his pilgrimage. He is extremely patient with the flighty and overemotional Margery. His kindness in continuing to share his meager income with her is phenomenal, especially in the face of her initial thoughtlessness in giving it away to the poor. Perhaps he is typically Irish in his powers of persuasion, as he convinces several groups of pilgrims to take care of Margery, who seems to have been an unwelcome member of more than one such party—she had previously been rejected by another group of pilgrims in Jerusalem. However, in portrayals of Irishmen or anything else, "Margery Kempe, so far as we can tell, exercised no influence at all," writes R. M. Wilson. "[U]ntil the modern discovery of her book she seems to have been known only by the fragments printed by Wynkyn de Worde, and these were hardly distinguishable from the ordinary religious literature of the period."[68]

6
Conclusions

In the course of this study, I have surveyed references to Ireland and the Irish in three major genres of Middle English literature: chronicles and other historical/political works; romances; and hagiography and religious/didactic works. In both chronicles and romances, the majority of such references appear in passages recounting the pseudo-historical conquest of Ireland by King Arthur. Among chronicles, the one exception in Ranulph Higden's *Polychronicon,* which quotes and summarizes extensively from Giraldus Cambrensis's *Historia et Topographia Hibernica,* and which may have been more influential than any of the other chronicles, since it was so widely known in both Latin and in two English translations. The main exception in romances are *King Horn* and *Horn Child* and the tale of Sir Tristram in verse *(Sir Tristrem)* and prose (Malory). In religious writings, the majority of references to Ireland are provided by *vitæ* of four saints—Brendan, Brigit, Cuthbert, and Patrick—along with two Irish visions, that of Sir Owain in *St. Patrick's Purgatory,* and the *Vision of Tundale.* The few references to Irish priests in the sermons of Mirk's *Festial* and in poetic debate and satire (*The Owl and the Nightingale* and *Piers Plowman*), suggest what contemporary ecclesiastical Latin sources make more explicit—that Irish friars and priests were considered insincere and less than diligent in caring for their spiritual flocks.[1]

The Limitations of Genre

The interpretation of this information about Ireland and the Irish in each of these types of literature depends in part on the different origins and purposes of each (loosely defined) genre. For example, consider the writers and audience of medieval chronicles: writers and translators of English and Latin chronicles dedicated their work to royal patrons, and thus tended to slant their accounts to please these aristocrats—Giraldus Cambrensis is a prime example (his works on Ireland and Wales were addressed to Henry II). Powerful monasteries such as St. Alban's, the home of Latin chroniclers Roger Wendover, Matthew Paris, and Thomas Walsingham, "retained the patronage of kings and princes. . . . Their abbots were dignified 'barons' of the realm, and they were in constant social touch with great affairs."[2] Chroniclers' interest in maintaining the goodwill of royal patrons often led to the writing of "official history," accounts that furthered the aims of the English realm. In addition, because such works were "assumed to be true (and for the most part accurate),"[3] especially when they refer to events within living memory, they would probably carry more force in forming the opinions of their audience.

Romances, on the other hand, were "the principal secular literature of entertainment of the Middle Ages."[4] Here the line between fact and fiction is often blurred (especially in the Arthurian romances, which may "have been believed to contain real history"[5]), and though patriotism may be an element (as it is in chronicles), it manifests itself differently, since the romance writer's imagination was freed from the need for "historical accuracy." Concerning one such romance, Jörg O. Fichte writes, "*Arthour and Merlin . . .* reflects political ideas and interests current in the 13th century. It is a document which recalls a former high point in English history, thereby promoting the formation of a distinctive English national consciousness and bolstering English claims to both the adjacent territories and the crown's possessions in France."[6] Jutta Wurster believes that the primary audience for such patriotism would have been "among the gentry and burgesses."[7] One would expect, then, that references to Ireland and the Irish in romances might both reveal and influence English imaginary archetypes of the island and its people—metaphors for the writers' and audience's emotional attitudes. Stephen Knight develops a similar hypothesis in his article, "The Social Function of the Middle English Romances," in which he defines the romances as a kind of

> "imaginary" [i.e., a "cultural product" that gives an] account of how people make use of and are controlled by a dominant ideology. . . . They are the best testimony to the hopes and fears of the medieval English ruling class, and a part of the cultural pressure on those who permitted them to rule. . . .[8]

In other words, art and life may have imitated each other more or less reciprocally.

Religious and didactic works reflect and support the interests of the church, in much the same way that chronicles supported secular political interests. Thus, the inclusion of certain saints' lives in legendaries partly reflects the veneration of these saints in English churches. At the same time, however, the choice probably also reflects the tastes of the lay audience, who could always be counted on to wake up for a good story—and the Irish saints and visions offered some of the best. Thus it seems significant that some Irish saints more or less disappear from English hagiography in Middle English, saints such as St. Aidan and St. Columkille, who were actually much more important to the preconquest English church. Although neither of these saints had much following in England after the seventh century, with the exception of Glastonbury and its associated monasteries,[9] they were at least known.[10] But their *vitæ* were never translated into Middle English, perhaps because they are not as strange, not as romantic, as Brendan's and Brigit's. (Even St. Patrick's life is curtailed in the Middle English legendaries, which focus instead on Sir Owain's vision in St. Patrick's Purgatory.) In light of the English church's interest in gaining control over the Irish church (reflected in policy as late as the fourteenth century, even after Canterbury's original claims to primacy in Ireland had lapsed[11]), another possible reason for the neglect of Aidan and Columkille in Middle English hagiography, is that these two Irish saints in particular played an important role in founding the early English church, a role that the postconquest English would want to play down, since they had come to view themselves as reformers of the Irish church.

The other factor that affects interpretation of references to Ireland and the Irish in Middle English is the limiting of the present study to vernacular texts. Obviously, literacy during the medieval period in England was not confined to the English language. French and Latin texts are much more numerous throughout the three centuries (1200–1500), and a truly comprehensive study would examine all these materials and doubtless reveal a much wider range of opinions on Ireland and the Irish. Even so, limiting the study to works in Middle English still means that almost all literate English persons are included in the (potential) audience except "at most the upper aristocracy and royal family, and those not after the mid-fourteenth century,"[12] and many illiterate ones, as well, if we accept the view that many of these works (especially the romances, saints' lives, and other religious/didactic materials) would have been at times read aloud.[13] The types of people likely to be literate grew increasingly diverse throughout the Middle English period, as well, as discussed in the Introduction. For example, D. W. Robertson, Jr., notes,

> The fact that peasants of villein status often sought and obtained fee permission to send off their sons to acquire sufficient education to enter the clergy suggests strongly . . . that small schools for boys conducted by priests, chaplains, monks, or canons were probably more numerous in rural areas than has been generally supposed, for the boys in question had probably shown some aptitude for elementary instruction. Some peasants, especially reeves . . . probably attended sessions of the shire courts, and in the general round of social activities that accompanied such sessions may have been exposed to some "literary" entertainment.[14]

On the other hand, while a formal education would certainly have included Latin and possibly French, by the end of the fourteenth century "three-quarters of the population could speak only English,"[15] so that only English works would have been suitable for reading aloud, except in the more exalted circles.[16] Also, much of the material in Latin which is now available to scholars must have been quite inaccessible to most English people, literate or otherwise—monastic chronicles and annals, government documents, and so forth. Thus, while the ideas about Ireland and the Irish that seem to emerge in Middle English literature cannot represent the entire range of opinions held by people living in England, they are the only images that would have been available to many of those who might have read or heard them.

History and Literature

In any case, historians who now have access to all these materials generally agree that when the Welsh-Normans and English invaded and settled in Ireland from the late twelfth century on, they found themselves confronted by a culture that was, in many ways, incompatible with their own. In England, as Otway-Ruthven explains in *A History of Medieval Ireland,* "by the later twelfth century the new Anglo-Norman society was already setting on lines which precluded that ready adoption of alien custom which had been so marked a feature of Norman conquest both in Wales and Italy."[17] As David Beers Quin notes, contrasting the two cultures:

> A stable land system, anchored by primogeniture, fitted the wheat- and vine-growing areas . . . of continental Europe and the English Low-

lands. The pastoral society of the western highlands and coast lands, with oats and barley grown where possible . . . was more flexible in its arrangements about land and was consequently looked down upon as being primitive and savage.[18]

In addition, the developing English "pattern of government" was based on a centralized monarchy.[19] This rather inflexible feudal culture met in Ireland a society which, according to Steven G. Ellis,

> comprised a series of autonomous lordships each with its own politics. . . . [A]mong the Gaelic chiefs there was almost no political cohesion at all, except when a few chiefs were briefly united by self-interest. . . . In terms of material culture, [Gaelic society] fell far short of the standards generally obtaining in western Europe. Militarily its weapons were outmoded, though the tactics of its chiefs were well-suited to the defence of the heavily-wooded, marshy or mountainous territory in which many of the Irish lived.[20]

Similarly, English monks bent on reforming the church in Ireland (and Scotland) "found . . . a Church which differed in many ways from their own, and, of course, a social context entirely outside their experience."[21]

The English often reacted with a mixture of fear and hostile superiority, as indicated by the stereotype of the "wild Irish," first found in the fourteenth-century vernacular prose chronicle *Brut*[22]—barbarous, treacherous, cruel, and (occasionally) heretical—in other words, a race that either deserved to be conquered as a form of retribution, or else needed to be conquered and civilized for their own good.

This view was not universal, however; witness William of Canterbury's comment on a certain Theobald, wounded in the Irish war. "It served him right, or so those thought who saw no reason for the disquieting of a neighbouring nation, who, however uncivilised and barbarous, were remarkable and noteworthy practisers of the Christian religion."[23] Similarly, the statement by William of Newburgh (chronicler of the reigns of Stephen, Henry II, and Richard I) that "what the Britons assert as to Ireland having been under the subjugation of their Arthur is merely fabulous"[24] shows that not everyone bought Giraldus Cambrensis's claim based on Geoffrey of Monmouth.[25]

Unfortunately, both of these dissenting views are found in Latin chronicles and apparently never made their way into Middle English. Nevertheless, to say that the English viewed the Irish as simply barbaric, as Snyder argued, is indeed oversimplified.

Instead, the "wild Irish" are but one of these distinct (though sometimes overlapping or interconnected) images of Ireland and the Irish which manifest themselves in the three general classes of literature surveyed. The other two are the Wasteland and the Otherworld Island, and are not necessarily either positive or negative, though they also reflect England's alienation from Ireland and the Irish.

The "Wild Irish"

First let us consider the stereotype of treacherous Irish barbarians, the "wild Irish." This image is found most frequently, and in most striking detail, in Middle English chronicles, annals, and political satires—and this is not surprising, considering the writers and audience of English and Latin chronicles. The concept of the "wild Irish" contributed to England's colonial aims by presenting the Irish as a group of people whose character, customs, language, and appearance are so barbaric that they could scarcely be perceived as fellow human beings. Thus to conquer them and try to educate and reform them could almost be viewed as a charitable act, rather than an imposition of political power.

However, political motives for portraying the Irish as savages were not necessarily premeditated, but grew from the usual reaction of almost any group upon encountering people with markedly different social customs. The language barrier intensified misunderstandings on both sides. Latin was a common language only for the learned members of both cultures and was confined to a small minority, mostly clergymen, who were often the most violently anti-Irish.[26] For example, Art Cosgrove gives an account of how Irish university students and priests in England were hounded as "wild Irish," often by their fellow clerics, in the first half of the fifteenth century.[27]

The Wasteland—Opportunity and Exile

Related to the concept of the "wild Irish" is the image of Ireland as Wasteland, that is, a region that is either uninhabited, or if it is inhabited, the land is mostly uncultivated (i.e., "unused"), and the natives are uncivilized, dangerous people. The first explicit reference appears in Geoffrey of Monmouth's account of how the British King Gurguintius sent Basque refugees to settle in an "uninhabited" Ireland; some version of this account is included in most Middle English chronicles. The view of the English might have been that if a land is uninhabited, or uncultivated—if no one is using it, or if the natives are not using it the way they would— why shouldn't they go in and show them how to farm? In chronicles this is seen in the *Polychronicon*'s glowing descriptions of Irish geography—for example, climate, topography, and flora and fauna (based on Bede and Giraldus)—and constrastingly deprecating accounts of how poorly the Irish use their land and how dreadfully they behave otherwise. One cannot help comparing this image of Ireland as wasteland to that of America or Australia in later English writings—a land of enormous potential, inhabited only by savages who weren't really using it anyway. In fact, the colonization of Ireland was a significant step in England's colonization of the New World which would begin and proceed rapidly in the sixteenth century. Bernard Bailyn writes:

> By 1604 Ireland and America were seen as equivalent centers of overseas expansion and they were linked geographically in Englishmen's minds. As they looked out at the world beyond England they saw a single arc of overseas territories suitable for colonization sweeping north and west from Britain, enclosing Ireland, Newfoundland, and the mainland coast of North America south to the Caribbean. It was therefore natural that nearby Ireland, which was described in a travel book of 1617 as "this famous island in the Virginia Sea," would be the first and primary object of colonization in the explosion of enterprise of the early seventeenth century.[28]

Quin notes in *The Elizabethans and the Irish,* that English explorers writing in the sixteenth and seventeenth centuries frequently compared Native American dress and customs to those of the Irish.[29]

The wasteland is also a traditional place of exile, religious or political, and Ireland had been a haven for political and religious exiles long before the Normans arrived, according to evidence from as far as back the eighth century (Bede 195).[30] However, in Middle English romances and chronicles, the exiles are all political, from King Horn to Guinevere (*Alliterative Morte Arthure* ll. 3907– 10) to Piers Gaveston, a historical figure in whose circumstances life seems to have echoed art (*Prose Brut,* I.206/20–22).[31] However, the land of exile is not necessarily a terrible place. King Horn, at least, found the Irish most welcoming, and their loyal support helps him regain his kingdom.

The Otherworld Island

The image of the Otherworld island is implied by references to Ireland and the Irish in Middle English chronicles, romances, and hagiography, suggesting that behind the assertions of superiority lay mystification in the face of an ancient tradition so alien that it was nearly incomprehensible to Norman/French-influenced English society. Traces of Irish mythology and folklore had already entered English traditions by a variety of routes and lent the English imagination of the island and its inhabitants, especially in romances, many qualities characteristic of the Otherworld, a realm where anything might happen. In general, Ireland as the Otherworld island in Middle English literature is not the glamorous, innocent Celtic Otherworld of birds, music, and beautiful women.[32] Rather, with its hostile inhabitants and mysterious places—giants, dragons, "enchanteors" (SEL *St. Brigit* 17–42), marvellous wells, lakes, and islands (*Polychronicon* I.361–65)—it is a dangerous, threatening place. And in religious works, for example, the Otherworld visions of Sir Owain and Tundale are more concerned with Hell and Purgatory than with Paradise.

The attractiveness of Ireland as an Otherworld island for Middle English writers and readers seems to me to lie primarily in two elements of the nature of Ireland itself as seen by the English. First, and most obviously, its location in the west across the Irish Sea fit many descriptions of Otherworld islands, as discussed in chapter 3. Second, and more important, is the relatively unknown, and therefore alien nature of Ireland and Irish culture from the English point of view. Despite ties between English and Irish monasteries as old as St. Patrick and St. Columkille, and perhaps equally ancient commercial trading,[33] it seems likely that by the late thirteenth century the ideas of many in England about Ireland came either directly or filtered from Giraldus Cambrensis's shocking twelfth-century accounts in *Expugnatio Hibernica* and *Topographia Hibernica,* ideas which continued to prevail primarily by way of Higden's *Polychronicon,* the most widely circulated chronicle of the fourteenth and fifteenth centuries. The bizarre aspects of the land and culture Giraldus describes must have seemed utterly alien to medieval English readers. Add the language barrier, and one finds a psychological distance between England and Ireland nearly as great as the physical distance between England and other, much more remote countries that also serve as Otherworldly settings for romantic adventures, such as Armenia, Arabia, or India—places most western European people had never seen, which might as well have been completely imaginary. As T. McAlindon points out:

> [T]he basic attraction of the journey (quest, or pilgrimage) to the Otherworld lies less in its example of heroism than in providing the vicarious pleasure of penetrating to a totally new realm of experience. In this way it answers something deeply rooted in human nature, the desire to escape from normality, to transcend the limitations of nature. . . .[34]

Thus, Ireland becomes an attractive site for magical adventures. And as a fictional locale in the minds of medieval English audiences (unlike some impossibly distant countries just mentioned) Ireland had the advantage of existing both in the verifiably real world and in the imaginary world of the readers' prejudices, fears, and desires, setting up a beguiling resonance between the fantastic events and beings described as Irish and the factual existence of an island one can easily visit from England—an island where there probably were no more giants or dragons, but who could say for sure?

Although Ireland's Otherworld qualities are seen most clearly in the romances, they are also recorded in chronicles, especially in the *Polychronicon,* and in religious writings, especially in the lives of Irish saints and in accounts of visions of the Christian Otherworld (e.g., *St. Patrick's Purgatory* and the *Vision of Tundale*).

The Otherworld component of these religious writings is especially interesting because the Christian subject matter covers it with a sanctified veneer. The result is that while the Irish saints are among the few praiseworthy Irish persons to be found in Middle English literature, they are also among the strangest (of any race). St. Brendan's voyage to the islands in the west is unique in European hagiography and though it taxed the credibility of some clerics,[35] it was nevertheless a very popular tale.[36] The remarkable manifestations surrounding the conceptions and births of Brigit and Cuthbert and their bizarre miracles echo the Irish mythology out of which they grew,[37] though the English audience was doubtless unaware of that folklore.

In considering the concept of Ireland as Otherworld island, it seems significant that of the fifteen visionary legends mentioned in the *Manual of Writings in Middle English,* five take place in Ireland or appeared to an Irishman. This is not to say that Middle

English writers or audiences actually equated the mythical Otherworld island with the Christian Hell/Purgatory/Heaven. Rather, the myth may have added to the plausibility of Irish visions and voyages (at least for the less critical readers or listeners). Thus, St. Brendan sets out from Ireland to reach the mysterious western isles, most of which have spiritual significance, and a gateway to Purgatory is revealed to St. Patrick in an Irish cave—combining the Otherworld island with the other traditional concept of the Otherworld underground.

The Real Ireland

There are, of course, exceptions to these stereotypes, such as the civilized, welcoming Irish people in *King Horn, Horn Childe,* and Malory's "Book of Sir Tristram." In addition, one finds occasional references to "the real Ireland," such as the reference to the musical expertise of the Irish in *Sir Tristrem*—Irish music seems to have been so popular among the Hiberno-English colonists that it was forbidden as subversive (along with intermarriage between English and Irish, speaking Gaelic, and playing Irish games) in the 1366 Statutes of Kilkenny.[38] References to the Irish pastoral economy and countryside in works such as the romance *Prose Merlin* (I.115) and the *Polychronicon* (I.333, 353) reflect a real knowledge of contemporary Ireland, as do references to the Hiberno-Norse settlers, though these are veiled by their romance settings (*Alliterative Morte Arthure* ll. 3932–36, cf. ll. 26–48, 3532; Lovelich's *Merlin* III.460) and by the fact that these people with Norse names are always called "Irish." The custom of fosterage was still practiced in Ireland as late as 1366 (when it was forbidden by the Statutes of Kilkenny,[39] though the extent to which the Statutes were enforced is open to question[40]), and is mentioned in the "Irish Life" of St. Cuthbert (ll. 385–88, 585–92) and in Laȝamon's *Brut* (II.11, 168–69). And the description of the Irish climate, flora, and fauna in the *Polychronicon,* based largely on Giraldus, is more or less accurate for its time, as far as I know (I.329–39). Thus, a certain amount of accurate, more or less neutral information about Ireland and Irish culture was available to the writers and audience of Middle English literature, but it seems to have been overwhelmed by the alienating, negative stereotypes. These literary concepts both reflected current attitudes, and influenced present and future English views of her neighboring island. Even harsher versions would come to dominate English portrayals of Ireland the Irish in the sixteenth and seventeenth centuries, as English efforts to establish dominance in Ireland intensified.[41]

Notes

Chapter 1. Introduction

1. David Beers Quin, *The Elizabethans and the Irish* (Ithaca: Cornell University Press, 1966).

2. The standard histories of medieval Ireland are Goddard Henry Orpen, *Ireland Under the Normans, 1169–1333,* 4 vols. (1911–20; reprint, Oxford: Clarendon Press, 1968); Edmund Curtis, *A History of Medieval Ireland from 1086–1513* (1938; reprint, London: Methuen and Co. Ltd., 1978); A. J. Otway-Ruthven, *A History of Medieval Ireland,* 2d ed. (1967; reprint London: Ernest Benn, 1980); and Art Cosgrove, ed., *Medieval Ireland 1169–1534,* vol. 2 of *A New History of Ireland* (Oxford: Clarendon Press, 1987). There are also a number of shorter works that focus on particular periods within that four-century span, such as Robin Frame's *Colonial Ireland, 1169–1369,* Helicon History of Ireland (Dublin: Helicon, 1981); or James Lydon, *Ireland in the Later Middle Ages* (Dublin: Gill and Macmillan, 1973).

3. Quin, *Elizabethans and the Irish,* 7.

4. E. D. Snyder, "The Wild Irish: A Study of Some English Satires Against the Irish, Scots, and Welsh," *Modern Philology* 17 (1920): 687–725.

5. F. X. Martin, "The Image of the Irish—Medieval and Modern—Continuity and Change," in *Medieval and Modern Ireland,* ed. Richard Wall (Totowa, N.J.: Barnes and Noble, 1988), 1–18.

6. Walter Ullmann, "On the Influence of Geoffrey of Monmouth in English History," in *Speculum Historiale Geschichte im Spiegel von Geschichtsschreibung und Geschichtsdeutung,* ed. C. Bauer, L. Boehm, and M. Müller (Freiburg: 1965) 276.

7. J. A. Burrow, *Medieval Writers and Their Work: Middle English Literature and Its Background 1100–1500* (Oxford: Oxford University Press, 1982), 26.

8. Ibid., 47.

9. Janet Coleman, *Medieval Readers and Writers: 1350–1400* (New York: Columbia University Press, 1981), 20–21.

10. Ibid., n. 283.

11. Ibid., 24.

12. Ibid., 30.

13. Ibid., 52.

14. Ibid., 50.

15. Ibid., 26.

16. Anne Middleton, quoted in J. A. Burrow, "Postscript," *Essays on Medieval Literature* (Oxford: Clarendon Press, 1984), 115.

17. Coleman, *Medieval Readers,* 56–57.

18. James Lydon, "The Middle Nation," in *The English in Medieval Ireland.* Proceedings of the first joint meeting of the Royal Irish Academy and the British Academy, Dublin, 1982, ed. James Lydon (Dublin: Royal Irish Academy, 1984).

19. Ibid., 2, 26.

20. For a detailed catalog of sources of Hiberno-English literature, see Angus McIntosh and M. I. Samuels, "Prolegomena to a Study of Mediæval Anglo-Irish," *Medium Ævum* 37 (1968): 1–11; a brief overview may be found in Alan Bliss, "Language and Literature," in *English in Medieval Ireland,* and a more detailed study in Bliss and Joseph Long, "Literature in Norman French and English to 1534," in *New History of Ireland,* 2:708–36.

21. Although *Medieval Ireland, 1169–1534* (vol. 2 of *New History of Ireland,* is the most comprehensive and most recent source, I have chosen to base this account primarily upon Otway-Ruthven, as the most concise and coherent source.

22. The English church played a role parallel to England's secular political involvement in Ireland. Sometimes the two furthered each other. Two particularly useful sources for the history of English-Irish church relations are *The Church in Early Irish Society* by Kathleen Hughes (Ithaca, N.Y.: Cornell University Press, 1966) for the period before 1200, and *The Church and the Two Nations in Medieval Ireland* (New York: Cambridge University Press, 1970), by J. A. Watt. I will treat this subject in more detail in chapter 4.

23. Giraldus Cambrensis, *Expugnatio Hibernica,* ed. and trans. A. B. Scott and F. X. Martin (Dublin: Royal Irish Academy, 1978); quoted in Martin, "Diarmait Mac Murchada and the Coming of the Anglo-Normans," in *Medieval Ireland 1169–1534,* vol. 2 of *New History of Ireland,* 50.

24. Martin, "Diarmait Mac Murchada," 50. According to Martin:

Most of the sources agree that Derbforgaill was a willing accomplice in the abduction. . . . The Annals of Clonmacnoise blame her brother . . . for persuading her to flee with Mac Murchada in retaliation for the harsh treatment she was receiving from her husband. . . . Whatever Derbforgaill's passion or personal motives may have been, there is little doubt that Mac Murchada acted in cold blood. . . . he was determined to level old scores with Ua Ruairc and was able to insult him publicly by the abduction when he raided Bréifne. He aggravated the insult by making no effort to prevent Toirrdelbach Ua Conchobair from bringing her back to Ua Ruairc the following year. ("Diarmait" 50)

25. Otway-Ruthven, *History,* 42.

26. Ibid., 46.

27. Ibid., 48. Pope Adrian, an Englishman, had long ago (1159) approved the English conquest of Ireland "'according to the right of inheritance'" for the purpose of converting the Irish, who were in fact Christians, but whose religious practices differed markedly in some ways from Continental churches under Rome (Ullmann, "On the Influence of Geoffrey of Monmouth in English History," 272–73). There is perhaps still some question regarding Pope Adrian's role in the English conquest of Ireland through the document called "Bull *Laudabiliter."* Edmund Curtis pointed out that "no mention is made of this all important document in [Irish] native records of that time" (27). On the other hand, more recently, Otway-Ruthven cites sources to support her statement that the bull's "authenticity has been shown to be unquestionable" (60). Whether it was authentic or not, it seems to have been relied upon as such by the English.

28. Otway-Ruthven, *History,* 50–51.

29. Ibid., 66.

30. Quoted in ibid., 66.

31. Ibid., 66–67.

32. Ibid., 79.

33. Cited in ibid, 81.

35. Ibid., 97.
36. James Lydon, "The Expansion and Consolidation of the Colony, 1215–54," in *Medieval Ireland 1169–1534*, vol. 2 of *New History of Ireland*, 168.
37. Martin, "Image of the Irish," 13.
38. Otway-Ruthven, *History*, 224–26.
39. Quoted in ibid., 235.
40. Ibid., 235–36.
41. Ibid., 237.
42. Quoted in ibid., 237.
43. Ibid., 252–59.
44. Ibid., 259–67.
45. Ibid., 267–69.
46. Ibid., 291–92.
47. Quoted in ibid., 291.
48. Ibid., 291–92.
49. Ibid., 293.
50. Ibid., 326.
51. Ibid., 327.
52. Ibid., 330.
53. Quoted in ibid., 333.
54. Ibid., 333.
55. Ibid., 339–40.
56. Ibid., 339–76.
57. Ibid., 387.
58. Ibid., 402–3.
59. Ibid., 403–4.
60. Ibid., 408.

Chapter 2. Ireland in Middle English Chronicles and Historical Poems

1. *Bede's Ecclesiastical History of the English People* [*Historia Ecclesiastica Gentis Anglorum*], ed. and trans. Bertram Colgrave and R. A. B. Mynors (Oxford: Oxford University Press, 1969); Geoffrey of Monmouth, *The History of the Kings of Britain* [*Historia Regum Britanniae*], trans. and ed. Lewis Thorpe (1966; New York: Viking Penguin, 1986); Gerald of Wales, *The History and Topography of Ireland* [*Historia et Topographia Hibernica*], trans. John J. O'Meara (1951; New York: Penguin Books, 1982); Giraldus Cambrensis, *Expugnatio Hibernica* [*The Conquest of Ireland*], ed. and trans. A. B. Scott and F. X. Martin (Dublin: Royal Irish Academy, 1978). Subsequent quotations from these works are cited parenthetically in the text.
2. One-hundred-eighteen extant manuscripts and nine fragments of Ranulph Higden's Latin version *Polychronicon*; fourteen extant manuscripts, and four fragments of John Trevisa's Middle English translation, plus at least one other Middle English translation (Edward Donald Kennedy, *Chronicles and Other Historical Writings*, vol. 8 of *A Manual of the Writings in Middle English 1050–1500*, ed. Albert E. Hartung [New Haven, Conn.: Archon Books, 1989], 2659).
3. Kennedy, *Chronicles* 2659.
4. William of Malmesbury, *Chronicle of the Kings of England* [*De Gestis Regum Anglorum*], ed. J. A. Giles (London: George Bell and Sons, 1904); Mat-

thew Paris, *Chronica Maiora,* ed. Henry Richards Luard, Rolls series 57 (7 vols.) (London: 1872–83).

5. *The English Conquest of Ireland,* an Hiberno-English Middle English translation of Giraldus's *Expugnatio Hibernica* (c. 1500) (Giraldus Cambrensis, *Expugnatio Hibernica,* ed. and trans. Scott and Martin [Dublin: Royal Irish Academy, 1978]).

6. Laȝamon, *Brut,* ed. G. L. Brook and R. F. Leslie, 2 vols., Early English Text Society (EETS), original series (o.s.), nos. 250,. 277 (New York: Oxford University Press, 1963, 1978); Robert of Gloucester, *The Metrical Chronicle of Robert of Gloucester,* 2 vols., ed. William A. Wright (London: 1887); "A Fifteenth-Century Prose Paraphrase of Robert of Gloucester's Chronicle," ed. Andrew D. Lipscomb (Ph.D. diss., University of North Carolina at Chapel Hill, 1990); *The Brut, or The Chronicles of England,* ed. Friedrich W. D. Brie, 2 vols., EETS, o.s., nos. 131, 136 (London: K. Paul, Trench, Trübner, 1906, 1908); Robert Mannyng of Brunne, *The Story of England,* 2 vols., ed. F. J. Furnivall, Rolls Series 87 (London: 1887); Ranulph Higden, *Polychronicon,* trans. John Trevisa, 9 vols., Rolls Series 14, eds. Churchill Babington and Joseph Rawson Lumby (London: 1874, 1876); John Capgrave, *Capgrave's Abbreuiacion of Cronicles,* ed. Peter J. Lucas, EETS, o.s., no. 285 (New York: Oxford University Press, 1983); William Caxton, *Caxton's Mirrour of the World,* ed. Oliver H. Prior, EETS, extra series (e.s.), no. 110 (New York: Oxford University Press, 1966). Subsequent quotations from these works are cited parenthetically in the text.

7. Thorpe, introduction to *History of the Kings of Britain* by Geoffrey of Monmouth, 12.

8. Janet Coleman, *Medieval Readers and Writers: 1350–1400* (New York: Columbia University Press, 1981), 50.

9. Although *De Excidio Britanniae* is not, strictly speaking, a chronicle, but was written as "a fierce denunciation of the rulers and churchmen of [Gildas's] day," its preface is "the only surviving narrative history of fifth century Britain" (Michael Winterbottom, historical introduction to *The Ruin of Britain and Other Works* by Gildas, History from the Sources [Totowa, N.J.: Rowman and Littlefield, 1978], 1).

10. Gildas, *The Ruin of Britain and Other Works* [*De Excidio Britanniae*], trans. and ed. Michael Winterbottom, History from the Sources (Totowa, N.J.: Rowman and Littlefield, 1978), sec. 14.1.

11. Ibid., sec. 16.1.

12. Nennius, *British History and The Welsh Annals* [*Historia Brittonum et Annales Cambriae*], ed. and trans. John Morris, History from the Sources (Totowa, N.J.: Rowman and Littlefield, 1980), 26. Subsequent quotations from this work are cited parenthetically in the text.

13. *The Anglo-Saxon Chronicle: A Revised Translation,* trans. and ed. Dorothy Whitelock (New Brunswick, N.J.: Rutgers University Press, 1961). Its references to Ireland and the Irish make no (semantic) distinction between Gaelic and Norse Irish (calling them all "Scots"), and are about evenly divided between *pro*—for example, "565. In this year the priest Columba came from Ireland to Britain, to instruct the Picts, and built a monastery on the island of Iona" (13) or "684. In this year Ecgfrith sent an army [among the Scots], and with it Briht his ealdorman, and they miserably injured and burnt God's churches (23)—and *con*— for example, 937: the Battle of Brunanburh (69–70).

14. *Lebor Gabála Érenn,* the Book of Invasions of Ireland, although Nennius's version is incomplete (R. Mark Scowcroft, "*Leabhar Gabhála,* part 1: The

Growth of the Text," *Eriu* 38 (1987): 83; R. Mark Scowcroft, *"Leabhar Gabhála,* part 2: The Growth of the Tradition," *Eriu* 39 (1988): 3, 53–54).

15. A name very close to the Irish form of the leader's name in *Lebor Gabála,* Partholón, "the Irish form of Bartholomaeus" (Scowcroft, "Tradition," 57).

16. A similar example of the manipulation of "official history" is cited by V. H. Galbraith: the Process of Scotland, an act by which Edward I claimed control of Scotland. "In 1290 and 1291, the king by royal writ ordered the monasteries of England to search their chronicles and send him transcripts of anything to the purpose." Some of the replies from the monasteries have been preserved, in which the abbots refer to passages from Geoffrey of Monmouth, the *Brut,* William of Malmesbury, and other sources, which might be used to support the King's claims over Scotland (V. H. Galbraith, "Historical Research in Medieval England," in *Kings and Chroniclers: Essays in English Medieval History* [London: The Hambledon Press, 1982], 11: 34–35).

17. Ullmann, "On the Influence of Geoffrey of Monmouth in English History," 267.

18. Ibid., 268.

19. Ibid., 272–73.

20. Geoffrey of Monmouth, *History of the Kings of Britain* [*Historia Regum*], 196ff. Subsequent quotations from this work are cited parenthetically in the text.

21. Another account of an English (or Anglo-Saxon) conquest of Ireland is found in Higden's *Polychronicon,* which tells how in the time of King Fedlimid, four hundred years after "þe firste Seynt Patryk,"

> Turgesius, duke and ledere of Norweyes, brouʒt þider Norwayes, and occupied þat lond, and made in wel many places many depe diches and castelles. . . . But Irische men reccheþ nouʒt of castelles; for þey taken wodes for castelles, and mareys and mores for castel diches. But at þe laste Turgesius deide by gile ful wyles and wrenches. And for Englische men seiþ þat Gurmundus wan Irlond, and . . . of Turgesius makeþ no mynde; and Irische men spekeþ of Turgesius, and knoweþ not of Gurmundus—þerfore it is [to] wetynge þat Gurmundus hadde i-wonne Bretayne, and wonde þerynne, and sente Turgesius wiþ grete strengþe of Bretouns in to Irlond forto wynne þat lond . . . þerfore Irische men spekeþ moche of hym as of a noble man þat was i-seie in Irlond and wel i-knowe in þat lond. . . . Turgesius loued þe kynges douʒter of Meth of Irlond; and hir fader behiʒt Turgesius, þat he wolde sende hir hym to þe Lowe Lacheryn wiþ fiftene maydenes; and Turgesius behiʒt for to mete him þere wiþ fiftene þe noblest men þat he hadde. He hyld couenant and þouʒt of no gile, but þere come fiftene ʒong berdles men i-cloþed as wommen, wiþ schorte swerdes vndir her cloþes, and fil on Turgesius and slowe hym riʒt þere. And so Turgesius was traytourliche i-slawe, after þat he hadde reigned þritty ʒere in þat lond. (I.347–9)

22. J. S. P. Tatlock, "Irish Costume in Lawman," *Studies in Philology* 28 (1931): 587–93.

23. Ibid., 56.

24. Gildas also describes this custom, which he ascribes to both the Irish and the Picts.

> They were to some extent different in their customs, but they were in perfect accord in their greed for bloodshed: and they were readier to cover their villainous faces with hair than their private parts and neighboring regions with clothes. . . . There was no respite from the barbed spears flung by their [the Britons'] naked opponents, which tore our wretched countrymen from the walls and dashed them to the ground. (sec. 19.1–4)

25. Tatlock, "Irish Costume," 58.

26. Tatlock, "Greater Irish Saints in Lawman and in England," *Modern Philology* 43 (1945–46): 72–76.

27. Ibid., 75.

28. Ibid., 74.

29. Donald G. Bzdyl, trans., introduction to *Layamon's Brut: A History of the Britons* (Binghamton, N.Y.: Medieval and Renaissance Texts and Studies, 1989), 10.

30. Ibid., 10.

31. F. X. Martin, "Diarmait Mac Murchada and the Coming of the Anglo-Normans," in *Medieval Ireland 1169–1534*, vol. 2 of *A New History of Ireland*, ed. Art Cosgrove (Oxford: Clarendon Press, 1987), 53.

32. A. B. Scott and Martin, introduction to *Expugnatio Hibernica* by Giraldus Cambrensis, ed. and trans. A. B. Scott and F. X. Martin (Dublin: Royal Irish Academy, 1978), xvii–xviii.

33. Ibid., xxvii.

34. Ibid., xxxiv–lii.

35. Giraldus's *Expugnatio Hibernica* was translated into Middle English about 1500 and exists in two Hiberno-English manuscripts, perhaps suggesting the stake the English colonists had in perpetuating the view of the Irish as "wild" barbarians as part of their renewed efforts to maintain control in Ireland in the sixteenth century. Geoffrey Keating, the seventeenth-century Irish historian, writes, "Every one of the new Galls who write on Ireland writes . . . in imitation of Cambrensis . . . because it is Cambrensis who is as the bull of the herd for them for writing the false history of Ireland, wherefore they had no choice of guide" (*History of Ireland,* quoted in John J. O'Meara, introduction to *The History and Topography of Ireland* by Gerald of Wales [New York: Penguin Books, 1951, 1982], 13).

36. Higden's paraphrase here actually glosses over Giraldus's original, wherein he compares the East and the West in general, concluding: "let the East, then, have its riches—tainted and poisoned as they are. The mildness of *our* climate alone makes up to us for all the wealth of the East" (*History* 55, italics mine). I interpret his reference to "our climate" to mean the climate of Britain, not just that of Ireland.

37. Cf. Giraldus, *History* 100–104.

38. Cf. Ibid., 101.

39. Cf. Ibid., 102.

40. Cf. Ibid., 91, 106–9, 112–16.

41. The Irish reputation for hot-temperedness seems to be at the root of the single specific reference to Ireland in the works of Chaucer, found in *The Romaunt of the Rose:*

> Wikkid-Tunge . . . was so full of cursed rage.
> It sat hym well of his lynage,
> For hym an Irish womman bar;
> His tunge was fyled sharp and squar,
> Poignaunt, and right kerving,
> And wonder bitter in spekyng
> (Geoffrey Chaucer, "The Romaunt of the Rose," in *The Works of Geoffrey Chaucer,* 2d. ed, ed. F. N. Robinson [Boston: Houghton Mifflin, 1957], ll. 3799–814.)

According to Robinson's note, the French text reads, "'Irese' (or 'iraise'), interpreted by some as 'Irish,' by others as the common adjective 'iroise,' 'angry, a virago.' Langlois [editor of the French poem] (I. n. 192) suggests that the French poet intended a pun on the two words (Robinson, ed., *Works of Geoffrey Chaucer*, n. 877), indicating that the stereotype of Irish irascibility was found in France as well as in England. Chaucer's translation obscures the French pun, but retains the sense that the Irish are easily angered and, as a result, sharp-tongued.

Donald R. Howard suggests that Chaucer may have visited Ireland at least once. "It may be (but there is no evidence) that for some part of these years [1360–68] he was with [Prince] Lionel in Ireland when Lionel was viceroy there" (Howard, *Chaucer: His Life, His Works, His World* [New York: E.P. Dutton, 1987], 74). Frederick R. Tupper argued that *Anelida and Arcite* is in fact a *roman à clef* concerning the marital troubles of James Butler, second Earl of Ormonde, and his wife, Anne Welle (Tupper, "Chaucer's Tale of Ireland," *PMLA* 36 (1921): 186–222). The evidence is thin and must be stretched even thinner to cover this hypothesis. As Robinson notes in his introduction to the poem:

> In the case of Butler the identification with Arcite rests entirely upon a few strange resemblances in proper names—Ormonde and Ermonie, Arcite and d'Arcy (Butler's mother's maiden name), Anelida and Anne Welle. . . . Ormonde's marital infidelity is by no means proved, and his life with the Countess was certainly not such as to justify his representation as the faithless Arcite. (Robinson, *Works* 303)

42. Coleman, *Medieval Readers* 50–51.

43. Cosgrove, "England and Ireland, 1399–1449," in *Medieval Ireland 1169–1534*, vol. 2 of *New History of Ireland*, 531.

44. V. J. Scattergood, *Politics and Poetry in the Fifteenth Century* (New York: Barnes & Noble, 1972), 192.

45. "The Twelve Letters to Save Merry England," in *Political, Religious, and Love Poems*, ed. F. J. Furnivall, EETS, o.s., no. 15 (London: K. Paul, Trench, Trübner, 1866; reedited, 1903), ll. 41–48.

46. Scattergood, *Politics and Poetry*, 191.

47. Otway-Ruthven, *History*, 387ff.

48. Henry Richards Luard, introduction to *Chronica Maiora* by Matthew Paris, ed. Henry Richards Luard, Rolls series 57 (7 vols.) (London: 1872–83), xxxii–xxxiii; Galbraith, "Historical Research," XI.34–5.

49. Otway-Ruthven, *History*, 97.

50. James Lydon, "The Expansion and Consolidation of the Colony, 1215–54," in *Medieval Ireland 1169–1534*, vol. 2 of *New History of Ireland*, 168.

51. See *Oxford English Dictionary* entry for "Irish," 5.B.1.a.

52. E. D. Snyder, "The Wild Irish: A Study of Some English Satires Against the Irish, Scots, and Welsh," *Modern Philology* 17 (1919–20): 377–381. The Hiberno-English "Libelle of englysshe polycye" [ca. 1436] refers to the Irish almost exclusively as "wylde Yrishe" (*Political Poems and Songs Relating to English Antiquity*, vol. 2, ed. Thomas Wright, Rolls Series 14 [London: 1859–61]).

53. James Lydon, "Richard II's Expeditions to Ireland," *The Journal of the Royal Society of Antiquaries of Ireland* 93, part 2 (1963): 135–49.

54. *Richard the Redeless*, ed. W. Skeat, EETS, o.s., no. 54 (London: 1873), ll. 9–10; Scattergood, *Politics*, 37.

55. This will be discussed in more detail in chapter 4. It is also related to the romance motif of Ireland as an Otherworld island (chap. 3).

56. John Lydgate, *The Sudden Fall of Princes*, in *Historical Poems of the*

XIVth and XVth Centuries, ed. Rossell Hope Robbins (New York: Columbia University Press, 1959), ll. 43–49.

57. Robbins, 343.

58. Or Phillippa (Robbins 343).

59. Compare a similar "Irish statute of Henry IV" which made "provisions against labourers leaving [Ireland]" (Kevin Down, "Colonial Society and Economy in the High Middle Ages," *Medieval Ireland 1169–1534,* vol. 2 of *New History of Ireland,* 449).

60. Cosgrove, "England and Ireland," 526.

61. Ibid., 528–29.

62. Martin, "Image of the Irish," 13.

63. Scattergood, *Politics and Poetry,* 114–15.

64. *Mum and the Sothsegger,* eds. Mabel Day and Robert Steele, EETS, o.s., no. 199 (London: H. Milford for Oxford University Press, 1936), Prologue ll. 8–12.

65. Scott and Martin, Introduction to *Expugnatio Hibernica,* xxix–xxx.

66. Eventually, the people of Calais repelled the Flemings, who abandoned the siege on 25 July. On 2 August, an English army arrived to relieve Calais. Finding this unnecessary, the leader, Gloucester, "made a brief harry into Flanders, and returned laden with loot" (Robbins, *Historical Poems,* 289).

67. "The Siege of Calais," in ibid., ll. 115–26.

68. Cf. Giraldus, *History,* 35.

69. Tatlock, "Greater Irish Saints," 74.

70. Scott and Martin, introduction to *Expugnatio Hibernica,* xxvii.

Chapter 3. Ireland and the Irish in Middle English Romances

1. Laȝamon, *Brut,* eds. G. L. Brook and R. F. Leslie, 2 vols., EETS, o.s., nos. 250, 277 (New York: Oxford University Press, 1963, 1978); *Of Arthoure and of Merlin,* ed. O. D. Macrae-Gibson, 2 vols., EETS, o.s., nos. 268, 279 (New York: Oxford University Press, 1973, 1979); *Sir Tristrem,* ed. George P. McNeill. Scottish Text Society 8 (1886; reprint. New York: Johnson Reprint Corp., 1966); *Lybeaus Desconus,* ed. M. Mills, EETS, o.s., no. 261 (London: Oxford University Press, 1969); *Morte Arthure or The Death of Arthur [Alliterative Morte Arthure]* ed. Edmund Brock, EETS, o.s. no. 8 (London: K. Paul, Trench, Trübner, 1871; reprint 1904); Thomas Chestre, *Sir Launfal,* ed. A. J. Bliss (London: Thomas Nelson and Sons, 1960); *Le Morte Arthure [Stanzaic Morte Arthure],* ed. J. Douglas Bruce, EETS, e.s., no. 88 (1903; reprint New York: AMS Press, 1979); Henry Lovelich, tran., *The History of the Holy Grail,* ed. F. J. Furnivall, EETS, e.s., no. 30 (London: 1878); Lovelich, *Merlin [Prose Merlin],* ed. Ernst A.Kock, 5 parts, EETS, e.s., nos. 93, 105, 112 (London: K. Paul, Trench Trübner, 1904–13), EETS, o.s. nos. 112, 185 (London: K. Paul, Trench, Trübner, 1899; H. Milford, Oxford University Press, 1932); *Merlin, or The Early History of King Arthur,* ed. Henry B. Wheatley, EETS, o.s., nos. 10, 21 (London: 1865, 1877); Thomas Malory, *Works,* ed. Eugène Vinaver, 2d ed. (New York: Oxford University Press, 1978; reprint 1981). Subsequent quotations from these works are cited parenthetically in the text.

2. *King Horn,* ed. Rosamund Allen, Garland Medieval Texts 7 (New York: Garland Publishing, 1984); *The Romance of Guy of Warwick,* part 2, ed. Julius Zupitza, EETS, e.s., no. 49 (London: 1887); "Horn Childe," in *King Horn: A*

Middle English Romance, ed. Joseph Hall (Oxford: Clarendon Press, 1901); *The Romans of Partenay, or of Lusignan,* ed. W. Skeat, EETS, o.s., no. 22 (London: K. Paul, Trench, Trübner, revised and reprint 1899). Subsequent quotations from these works are cited parenthetically in the text.

3. Mills, ed., *Lybeaus Desconus,* n. 238.

4. George P. McNeill, ed., introduction to *Sir Tristrem,* 99.

5. A similar reference to Ireland appears in the thirteenth-century lyric, "A Hymn to Mary":

> Betere is hire medycyn
> Then eny mede or eny wyn;
>
> Hire erbes smulleth suete.
> From Catenas in to Dyvelyn
> Nis ther no leche so fyn
> Our serewes to bete. . . .
> (In *Early English Lyrics: Amorous, Divine, Moral, and Trivial,* eds. E. K. Chambers and F. Sidgwick [London: Sidgwick and Jackson Ltd., 1966], 98)

Here, Dublin is the other end of a sweeping length of the earth. I've not yet been able to identify "Catenas," except to tentatively suggest either Caithness, in Scotland, or Catania, in Sicily. In any case, this is another example of Ireland as the western end of the known world.

6. One-hundred-eighteen extant manuscripts and nine fragments of Ranulph Higden's Latin version; fourteen extant manuscripts, and four fragments of Trevisa's Middle English translation, plus at least one other Middle English translation (Kennedy 2659).

7. H. R. Patch, *The Other World According to Descriptions in Medieval Literature,* Smith College Studies in Modern Languages, new series, 1 (Cambridge, Mass.: 1950), passim.

8. Sometimes both, as in *St. Patrick's Purgatory.*

9. T. McAlindon, "The Treatment of the Supernatural in Middle English Legend and Romance, 1200–1400 (Ph.D. diss., Fitzwilliam House, Cambridge University, 1961), 108.

10. Patch, *Other World,* 8.

11. Ibid., 322.

12. T. F. O'Rahilly, *Early Irish History and Mythology* (Dublin: Institute for Advanced Studies, 1946), 493.

13. H. R. Patch, "The Adaptation of Otherworld Motifs to Medieval Romance," In *Philologica, the Malone Anniversary Studies,* eds. Thomas A. Kirby and Henry Bosley Woolf (Baltimore: Johns Hopkins University Press, 1949), 116.

14. Alwyn Rees and Brinley Rees, *Celtic Heritage: Ancient Tradition in Ireland and Wales* (1961; reprint London: Thames and Hudson, 1989), 297–313.

15. Patch, "Adaptation," 116.

16. Proinsias Mac Cana, *Branwen Daughter of Llyr* (Cardiff: University of Wales Press, 1958), 146–49.

17. Patch, *Other World,* 81. The Hiberno-English satire, "The Land of Cokaygne," incorporates a number of these Otherworld motifs, including its location, "Fur in see bi west Spayngne" (1). For a detailed study, see P. L. Henry, "The Land of Cokaygne: Cultures in Contact in Medieval Ireland." *Studia Hibernica* 12 (1972): 120–41; and Juliette de Caluwé-Dor, "L'Elément Irlandais dans la version moyen-anglais de The Land of Cockaygne," in *Mélanges de Langue et Littérature*

Françaises du Moyen Age et de la Renaissance offerts à Charles Foulon Rennes: Institut de Français, Universite de Haute-Bretagne, 1980, 1:89–98.

18. Thomas Malory, "The Book of Sir Tristram de Lyones," in *Works,* 2d ed., ed. Eugène Vinaver (New York: Oxford University Press, 1978; reprint 1981), 232–44. Subsequent quotations from Malory's *Works* are cited parenthetically in the text.

19. Patch, "Adaptation," 116.

20. "Ich am of Irlaunde," ed. John Speirs, in *Medieval English Poetry: The Non-Chaucerian Tradition* (London: Faber and Faber, 1957), 60–61.

21. Richard Leighton Greene, *The Early English Carols* (Oxford: Clarendon Press, 1935), xxxvii.

22. Speirs, *Medieval English Poetry,* 59–60.

23. Ibid., 60–61.

24. J. A. Burrow's analysis is somewhat more down-to-earth. He describes the sort of dance that might have accompanied "Ich am of irlaunde."

> The Irish speaker . . . would inevitably be identified with the soloist (herself presumably female), [so] we must imagine that the other dancers are, as it were, echoing her words in their burden. Perhaps the dance took the form of a Ladies' Excuse Me, with the soloist singling out whichever man stopped opposite her, when the ring of carollers had finished dancing round as she sang her stanza. In that case, she may have repeated the same stanza at each invitation. Otherwise, the text must be fragmentary (Burrow, "Poems Without Contexts: The Rawlinson Lyrics," in *Essays on Medieval Literature* [Oxford: Clarendon Press, 1984], 13–14)

Burrow argues that it is not necessary to assume a mysterious "ritual" context for the song. For the medieval dancers, he speculates,

> It may have been enough for them to identify "Ireland", in the make-believe geography of the dance floor, with the area occupied by the soloist at the centre of the ring of carollers. The symbolism of dance would then quite naturally explain why this area represented a "holy land" ("Weave a circle round him thrice"). (Ibid., 14)

25. The earliest "historical" accounts of Irish monsters are cited by Giraldus Cambrensis, who writes of bizarre creatures such as werewolves, a bearded woman, and a man who "had all the parts of the human body except the extremities. . . . From the joining of the hands with the arms and the feet with the legs, he had hooves the same as an ox" (69–73).

26. Darryl F. Lane, "An Historical Study of the Giant in the Middle English Metrical Romances" (Ph.D. diss., University of New Mexico, 1972), iv.

27. T. McAlindon, "The Emergence of a Comic Type in Middle English Narrative: The Devil and Giant as Buffoon," *Anglia* 81 (1962): 368.

28. From *The Battle of Maldon:*

> Hi bugon þā fram beaduwe   þe þǣr bēon noldon:
> þǣr wurdon Oddan bearn   ǣrest on flēame,
> Godrīc fram gūþe,   and þone gōdan forlēt;
> . . . .
> Godwine and Godwig,   gūþe ne gȳmdon,
> ac wendon fram þām wige,   and þone wudu sōhton,
> flugon on þæt fæsten,   and hyra fēore burgon,
> . . . .
> Swā him Offa on dæg   ǣr āsǣde,
> on þām meþel stede,   þā hē gemōt hæfde,

þæt þær mōdiglīce   manega spræcon,
þe eft æt þearfe   þolian nolde.
(*Two of the Saxon Chronicles Parallel*, rev. and ed. Charles Plummer
[Oxford: Clarendon Press, 1892], ll. 185–201)

(Then they who were not minded to be there retired from the battle. There the sons of Odda were the first in flight; Godric fled from the battle and left the valiant one. . . . [Godwine] and Godwig . . . cared not for war, but they turned from the fight and sought the wood; they fled to that fastness and saved their lives. . . . Thus erstwhile Offa once said to him in the meeting-place, when he held assembly, that many spoke bravely there who would not endure in [time of need]. [R. K. Gordon, trans., *Anglo-Saxon Poetry* (London: J.M. Dent, 1954; reprint 1959), 332].)

29. On the basis of this description it has been suggested that Ireland is the rugged country referred to by the Nightingale in *The Owl and the Nightingale*, ll. 999–1014 (Kathryn Huganir, *The Owl and the Nightingale: Sources, Date, Author* [Philadelphia: University of Pennsylvania, 1931], 99, 106–9; E. G. Stanley, *The Owl and the Nightingale* [London: Thomas Nelson and Sons, 1960], n. 128). However, Giraldus later adds details that contradict some of the features of the passage (particularly regarding the cold climate) and help to clarify the identity of the land where nightingales do not sing.

Þat lond nis god, ne hit his este,
Ac wildernisse hit is & weste:
Knarres & cludes houentinge,
Snou and haȝel hom is genge;
Þat lond is grislich & unuele.
Þe men boþ wilde & unisele,
Hi nabbeþ noþer griþ ne sibbe.
Hi ne reccheþ hu hi libbe:
Hi eteþ fihs an flehs unsode
Suich wulues hit hadde tobrode,
Hi drinkeþ milc & wei þarto—
Hi nute elles wat hi do;
Hi nabbeþ noþ[er] win ne bor,
Ac libbeþ also wilde dor;
Hi goþ bitiȝt mid ruȝe uelle,
Riȝt suich hi comen ut of helle.
Þeȝ eni god man to hom come—
So wile dude sum from Rome—
For hom to lere gode þewes,
An for to leten hore unþewes,
Hi miȝte bet sitte stille,
Vor al his wile he sholde spille:
He miȝte bet teche an bore
To weȝe boþe sheld & spere,
Þan me þat wilde folc ibringe
Þat hi me wolde ihere singe.

Stanley cited several critics who noted similarities between this description and several medieval accounts of Scandinavia (n. 128) He also points out that Giraldus's description of Ireland also resembles the description in the poem. I would say that the identification with Norway is more likely. The main similarity to Giraldus's account of Ireland and the Irish is in the description of the people. "Þe men boþ wilde & unisele, / Hi nabbeþ noþer griþ ne sibbe. / Hi ne reccheþ hu hi libbe" (ll. 1004–6) and "Hi drinkeþ milc & wei þarto" (ll. 1009). However, Giraldus does not say that the Irish typically eat raw meat or dress in furs (ll. 1007, 1013), with the possible exception of two particularly backward specimens from the wilds of Connacht.

> Their hair was very long and flaxen, coming down and across their shoulders, as is the Irish manner, and covering most of their bodies. . . . They said that they fed only on meat, fish, and milk. They did not usually wear clothes, but sometimes in great necessity they used the hides of animals. (*History* 111)

Another possible similarity between the people described by the nightingale and the Irish as described by Giraldus is their ignorance of religion (ll. 1015–24). Although he acknowledged that Christianity had long been established in Ireland, Giraldus said of the Irish: "This is a filthy people, wallowing in vice. Of all peoples it is the least instructed in the rudiments of the Faith. . . . They do not attend God's church with due reverence" (*History* 106).

On the other hand, Giraldus's description of Ireland itself is generally quite attractive, and certainly "snou and haʒel" are not typical Irish weather. In fact, according to Giraldus:

> This is the most temperate of all countries. . . . You will seldom see snow here, and then it lasts only for a short time. . . . The grass is green in the fields in winter, just the same as in summer. . . . The country enjoys the freshness and mildness of spring almost all the year round. (*History* 53)

30. A parallel description of Ireland may be found in a fourteenth-century French romance by Froissart, *Meliador*, in which "Ireland is depicted . . . as a land largely covered with forests, where castles are few and far between and the road leading from the Clarense [River, which replaces the Irish sea here as the boundary between England and Ireland] to Dublin is so overgrown that the hero loses his way" (A. H. Diverres, "The Irish Adventures in Froissart's Meliador," Publications Romanes et Françaises 112, *Mélanges de langue et de Littérature du Moyen Age et de la Renaissance, Offerts à Jean Frappier* (Geneva: Librarie Droz, 1970), 235–51). The works of Froissart were, of course, well-known in England, and he himself had spent ten years "as 'clerc de la chambre' to Queen Philippa at Edward III's court" (Ibid., 235), during which time Edward III, "perturbed by the hibernicization of many Anglo-Irish nobles" (Ibid., 250), attempted by various means to gain greater control over the English territory in Ireland. According to Diverres, "The Irish adventures in *Meliador* are intended to depict an Irish aristocracy hostile to cultural and possible political influences from England, and a royal government concerned only with the welfare of Ireland" (Ibid., 251).

31. See chaps. 1, 2.

32. McKeehan notes this name as one of several "specific resemblances between the Cuthbert legend and the Horn saga" (Irene Pettit McKeehan, "Some Relationships Between the Legends of British Saints and the Medieval Romance," in *Abstracts of Theses/Humanistic Series* [University of Chicago] [Chicago: University of Chicago Press, 1926], 389–90). See chapter 4.

33. Valerie Krishna, introduction to *The Alliterative Morte Arthure* (New York: Burt Franklin, 1976), 12.

34. Karl Heinz Göller, "Reality versus Romance: A Reassessment of the Alliterative Morte Arthure," in The Alliterative Morte Arthure: *A Reassessement of the Poem,* ed. Göller (Cambridge: D.S. Brewer, 1981), 17.

35. R. E. Glasscock, "Land and People, c. 1300," in *Medieval Ireland 1169–1534*, vol. 2 of *A New History of Ireland*, ed. Art Cosgrove (Oxford: Clarendon Press, 1987), 226.

36. J. A. Watt, "Gaelic Polity and Cultural Identity," in *Medieval Ireland,* 331.

37. The incident is first recorded in the *Anglo-Saxon Chronicle* for the year 1049. The Old English version reads: "On þam ilcan geare comon upp on Wylisce Axa of Yrlande xxxvi, scypa. 7 þær abuton hearmas dydon mid Gryfines fultume þæs Wæliscan kynges (*Two of the Saxon Chronicles Parallel* 170; "In the same year thirty-six ships came up the Usk from Ireland and did damage in those parts with the help of Griffith, the Welsh king [*The Anglo-Saxon Chronicle,* Dorothy Whitelock, ed. and trans. (New Brunswick, N.J.: Rutgers University Press, 1961), D.114]).

Chapter 4. Ireland and the Irish in Saints' Lives

1. Gearóid Mac Niocaill, *Ireland Before the Vikings* (Dublin: Gill and Macmillan, 1972), 22.

2. Ibid., 24.

3. *Bede's Ecclesiastical History of the English People,* ed. and trans. Bertram Colgrave and R. A. B. Mynors (Oxford: Oxford University Press, 1969). Subsequent quotations from this source are cited parenthetically in the text.

4. Kathleen Hughes, *The Church in Early Irish Society* (Ithaca, N.Y.: Cornell University Press, 1966), 260.

5. James F. Kenney, *The Sources for the Early History of Ireland, Vol. 1: Ecclesiastical* (1929; rev. Ludwig Bieler, 1966; reprint Dublin: Pádraic Ó Táilliúir, 1979), 747.

6. Ibid., 746.

7. Ibid.

8. J. A. Watt, *The Church and the Two Nations in Medieval Ireland* (New York: Cambridge University Press, 1970), 6.

9. Ibid., 2.

10. Ibid., 38.

11. Kenney, *Sources,* 757.

12. Denis Bethell, "English Monks and Irish Reform in the Eleventh and Twelfth Centuries," *Historical Studies* 8, papers read before the Irish Conference of Historians, 27–30 May 1969 (Dublin: Gill and Macmillan, 1971), 116–18.

13. William of Malmesbury, *Memorials of St. Dunstan,* ed. William Stubbs, Rolls Series 63 (London: 1874), 257; trans. Bethell, 118.

14. "Cambrai Homily," *Thesaurus Palaeohibernicus,* vol. 2, ed. Whitley Stokes (Dublin: Dublin Institute for Advanced Studies, 1975), 246.

15. Kenney, *Sources,* 757.

16. Marie Therese Flanagan, *Irish Society, Anglo-Norman Settlers, Angevin Kingship: Interactions in Ireland in the Late Twelfth Century* (Oxford: Clarendon Press, 1989), 49.

17. Martin, "Diarmait," 52.

18. Ibid., 51.

19. Otway-Ruthven, *History,* 52–53.

20. Watt, *Church,* 72.

21. Ibid., 83.

22. Louis Gougaud, *Les Saints irlandais hors d'Irlande: Etudiés dans le culte*

et dans la dévotion traditionelle, Bibliothèque de la Révue d'Histoire Ecclésiastique (Oxford: Blackwell, 1936).

23. Gougaud; also John Hennig, "The Place of Irish Saints in Mediaeval English Calendars," *The Irish Ecclesiastical Record,* 5th ser., August 1954: 93–106.

24. Hennig, "The Place of Irish Saints in Late Mediaeval English Hagiography," *Medieval Studies* 16 (1954): 165.

25. Ibid.

26. Hennig, "Place of Irish Saints in Medieval English Calendars," 105–6.

27. Hennig, "The Place of Irish Saints in Late Medieval English Hagiography," 167.

28. Ibid., 168. According to Hennig, even Irish church calendars from this period "show strong English influence" ("Place of Irish Saints Mediaeval English Calendars," 105).

29. "A possible route to Rome for someone travelling from southern Ireland would have crossed the Irish sea from Wexford or Waterford to the Severn, and then passed by way of Glastonbury and Winchester to Canterbury" (Robinson, cited by Michael Lapidge, "The Cult of St. Indract at Glastonbury," in *Ireland in Early Medieval Europe,* eds. Dorothy Whitelock, Rosamund McKitterick, and David Dumville [New York: Cambridge University Press, 1982], n. 205).

30. Hennig, "Place of Irish Saints in Medieval English Calendars," 103. The shrine of St. Thomas Becket also attracted Irish pilgrims to Canterbury in the twelfth century.

> The most striking was Connor, *cognatus* to the High King Rory O'Connor, who suffered from elephantiasis and on the advice of a certain Abbot Marianus, made two pilgrimages to Canterbury to cure it. There were humbler pilgrims as well—a poor Irish boy called Colum who begged silver from the monks of Canterbury, and then stole a bottle to hold the holy water poured over the saint's bones; he confessed the sin to an Irish deacon (after he had got an appalling tumour on the neck) and did penance at the shrine. There was Sihtric from the central region of Ireland, who suffered from dropsy and redness of the nose, to whom St. Thomas personally appeared in Canterbury cathedral and spoke with in the Irish language. [Bethell, "English Monks," 124–25)

31. Bethell, "English Monks," 116–17.

32. Hennig, "Place of Irish Saints in Medieval English Calendars," 101.

33. Madeleine Hope Dodds, ed. and trans., "The Little Book of the Birth of St. Cuthbert, Commonly Called the Irish Life of St. Cuthbert," *Archaeologia Aeliana: or, Miscellaneous Tracts Relating to Antiquity,* 4th ser., 6 (1929): 58–59.

34. Laurence of Durham noted in his Latin version of the *Libellus,* "We have heard some of the greatest men, and not a few Irish bishops perorate on the Irish birth of St. Cuthbert . . . St. Malachy told King David of Scotland many things on this matter, and Maurilius his successor afterwards confidently asserted it and Eugenius bishop of Ardmore discussed it more exactly, and so did two other bishops whose names have been forgotten, and so did their companions, priests and clerks at various times" (quoted in Bethell, *"English Monks,"* 123).

35. Dodds, "Little Book," 63–64; see also J. T. Fowler, preface to *The Life of St. Cuthbert in English Verse, c. A.D. 1450, from the original MS in the library at Castle Howard,* Surtees Society 87 (Edinburgh: 1891), vi.

36. O. S. Pickering, "An Early Middle English Verse Inscription from Shrewsbury," *Anglia* 106, nos. 3–4 (1988): 412.

37. Ibid., 413.

38. Ibid., 414.

39. Ibid., 413.

40. Lapidge, "Cult," 183.

41. Ibid.

42. Ibid., 179.

43. William of Malmesbury, *Chronicle of the Kings of England* [*De Gestis Regum Anglorum*] ed. J. A. Giles (London: George Bell and Sons, 1904), 24–25. Subsequent quotations from this work are cited parenthetically in the text.

44. Lapidge, "Cult," 183.

45. Ibid., 184.

46. Clark H. Slover, "William of Malmesbury's *Life of St. Patrick*," *Modern Philology* 24 (1926): 20.

47. Kenney, *Sources,* 307; 606–8.

48. *The Early South English Legendary, or Lives of Saints (ESEL),* ed. Carl Horstmann, EETS, o.s., no. 87 (London: 1887). Subsequent quotations from this work are cited parenthetically in the text.

49. *The South English Legendary (SEL),* eds. Charlotte D'Evelyn and Arna J. Mill, vol. 1., EETS, o.s., no. 235 (London: Oxford University Press, 1956). Subsequent quotations from this work are cited parenthetically in the text.

50. Simon Lavery, "The Source of the St. Brendan Story in the South English Legendary," *Leeds Studies in English,* new ser., 15 (1984): 28–29. The editor Carl Selmer considers the poem to have been composed in Lotharingia, a province "which in the tenth century stretched from the present Lorraine northwards along the shore of the Rhine to the Low Lands and the Channel . . . the territory in which the Scotti had developed their noteworthy educational and literary activities" (Selmer, introduction to Navigatio Sancti Brendani Abbatis *from Early Latin Manuscripts* [Notre Dame, Ind.: University of Notre Dame Press, 1959], xxviii–xxix); more recently Orlandi has placed the composition of the *Navigatio* in early ninth-century Ireland (Orlandi, *Navigatio Sancti Brendani: Introduzione* [Milan, 1968], cited in Lavery, "Source," 21), as did Kenney (*Sources,* 415).

51. Latin *vitæ* of St. Dunstan, including one by William of Malmesbury, note that he studied extensively with Irish scholars at Glastonbury (*Memorials of St. Dunstan,* 10–11, 74–75, 256–57).

52. Charlotte D'Evelyn and Frances A. Foster, "Saints' Legends," in *A Manual of the Writings in Middle English,* ed. J. Burke Severs (Conn.: Academy of Arts and Sciences, 1970), 2: 416.

53. A number of exceeded by only three other texts: *The Prick of Conscience,* the *Canterbury Tales,* and *Piers Plowman* (in ibid., 416).

54. Hennig, "Place of Irish Saints in Medieval English Calendars," 104.

55. E. G. Bowen, "The Cult of St. Brigit," *Studia Celtica* 8–9 (1973–74): 39.

56. Ibid., 36.

57. Robert Easting, "Owein at St. Patrick's Purgatory" *Medium Ævum* 55, no. 2 (1986): 159.

58. Tatlock, "Greater Irish Saints," 73.

59. However, Higden's *Polychronicon,* a later fourteenth-century chronicle, notes about Ireland: "Dicta est etiam aliquando Scotia as Scotis eam inhabitantibus, priusquam ad alima Scotiam Britannicam devenirent. Unde in Martyrologio legitur: 'Tali die apud Scotiam Sanctæ Brigidæ;' quod est, apud Hiberniam" (I.330).

60. Kenney, *Sources,* 361.

61. Alwyn Rees and Brinley Rees, *Celtic Heritage: Ancient Tradition in Ireland and Wales* (New York: Thames and Hudson, 1961; reprint 1989), 213–19.

62. Ibid., 224.

63. Liam Mac Mathúna, "On the Expression and Concept of Blindness in Irish," *Studia Hibernica* 19 (1979): 55–58.

64. Selmer, Navigatio, xxviii, xxxi.

65. Joseph Dunn, "The Brendan Problem," *The Catholic Historical Review* 6, no. 4 (1921): 468.

66. Ibid., 465–67.

67. James F. Kenney, "The Legend of St. Brendan," in *Proceedings and Transactions of the Royal Society of Canada, 3d ser., 14 (1920): 55.*

68. Selmer, Navigatio, xxi; Patch, *Other World,* passim.

69. Thomas Wright, *St. Brandan: A Medieval Legend of the Sea in English Verse and Prose,* Percy Society 14 (London: 1844), 129.

70. Kenney, "Legend," 51.

71. Ibid.

72. *An Alphabet of Tales,* ed. Mary McLeod Banks, EETS, o.s., nos. 126–27 (London: K. Paul, Trench, Trübner and Co., 1904–5). Subsequent quotations from this work are cited parenthetically in the text.

73. Fowler, *Life of St. Cuthbert.* Subsequent quotations from this work are cited parenthetically in the text.

74. Dodds, "Little Book," 59.

75. Ibid., 59–60.

76. Bertram Colgrave, ed. *Two Lives of St. Cuthbert: A Life by an Anonymous Monk of Lindisfarne and Bede's Prose Life* (Cambridge: The University Press, 1940), 310, 315, passim. Another example of intermingled Irish and English saints is the Life of St. Modwenna of Burton-on-Trent, an English saint, which incorporates material from the Life of the Irish St. Modwenna of Killeavy by Conchubranus (Bethell, "English Monks," 122–23).

77. Dodds, "Little Book," 63.

78. Ibid.

79. Ibid.

80. Fowler, *Life of St. Cuthbert,* vi; Dodds, "Little Book," 62.

81. Irene Pettit McKeehan, "The Book of the Nativity of St. Cuthbert," *PMLA* 48, no. 4 (1933): 982.

82. Fowler, *Life of St. Cuthbert* vii.

83. Charles Eyre, *The History of St. Cuthbert,* 3d ed. (New York: 1887), 5.

84. Eyre suggests "'illustrious for skill'; or Guthbert, 'worthy of God,' or 'a good prince'" (ibid., 5).

85. Quoted in Eyre, *History of St. Cuthbert,* 4.

86. St. Lugaid of Lismore, of whom the story was originally told, died in A.D. 592 (Dodds, "Little Book," 60)—in other words, he *could* have been acquainted with St. Columba, and possibly even with St. Brigit. For further analysis of anachronisms, see Bollandists, *Acta Sanctorum,* Martii, 3:117.

87. Fowler, *Life of St. Cuthbert,* vi–vii.

88. Colgrave, *Two Lives of St. Cuthbert,* 5.

89. Dodds notes: "Reginald of Durham, who wrote c. 1175, about twenty years before the Libellus, that John, abbot of Furness, in the reign of Henry II won a law suit through the intervention of St. Cuthbert; in gratitude for this help, he dedicated an altar of St. Cuthbert in the abbey church and made a pilgrimage to Durham. St. Cuthbert, therefore, was particularly revered at Furness" (62).

90. McKeehan, "Book," 987–99.

91. Dodds notes: "Muriadach might stand for Muircheartach Mac Erc, who

was ard-righ of all Ireland, about the beginning of the sixth century. . . . Sabina is a latinized form of the Celtic Sadhbh, which was the name of at least one Irish legendary heroine" (66).

92. Fowler, *Life of St. Cuthbert,* 11.

93. Ibid., 2.

94. Dodds, "Little Book," 76.

95. Ibid., 68–69.

96. Glasscock, "Land and People," 226; J. A. Watt, "Gaelic Polity and Cultural Identity," in *Medieval Ireland 1169–1534,* vol. 2 of *A New History of Ireland,* ed. Art Cosgrove (Oxford: Clarendon Press, 1987), 331.

97. Dodds, *Little Book* 71–73.

98. Bergin, Osborn, "White Red-Eared Cows," *Ériu* 14, part 2 (1946): 170.

99. Fowler, *Life of St. Cuthbert,* 13.

100. Dodds, "Little Book," 75.

101. Rees and Rees, *Celtic Heritage,* 252.

102. Ibid.

103. Ibid., 252–53.

104. Ibid., 218–22.

105. McKeehan, "Book," 988.

106. Ibid.

107. Dodds, "Little Book," 70.

108. McKeehan, "Book," 995.

109. Ibid., 989–90.

110. Ibid., 990–91.

111. Rees and Rees, *Celtic Heritage,* 317. Like Sir Tristrem (see Romances chapter), St. Blane's boat lands in Ireland.

112. McKeehan, "Book," 991.

113. Fowler, *Life of St. Cuthbert,* 22.

114. Dodds, *Little Book,* 80.

115. Rees and Rees, *Celtic Heritage,* 315, 343.

116. Ibid., 315.

117. Dodds, *Little Book,* 80.

118. Ibid., 86–94. The antifemale bias was evidently introduced by the Normans, who invented explanations for changing the more liberal view of women in Celtic and Anglo-Saxon culture (Dodds, *Little Book,* 92).

Chapter 5. Ireland and the Irish in Visions of the Otherworld and Other Religious and Didactic Writings

1. Rees and Rees, *Celtic Heritage,* 314, 342–43.

2. Robert Easting, "The Date and Dedication of the *Tractatus de Purgatorio Sancti Patricii," Speculum* 53 (1978): 782.

3. Rodney Mearns, introduction to *The Vision of Tundale,* ed. Mearns, Middle English Texts 18 (Heidelberg: Carl Winter, 1985), 7.

4. Robert Mannyng of Brunne, *Robert of Brunne's* Handlyng Synne *And Its French Original,* ed. F. J. Furnivall, EETS, o.s., nos. 119, 123 (1901–3; reprint Millwood, N.Y.: Kraus Reprint Co., 1975, 1976); *An Alphabet of Tales,* ed. Mary MacLeod Banks, EETS, o.s., nos. 126–127 (London: K. Paul, Trench, Trübner, 1934). Subsequent quotations from these works are cited parenthetically in the text.

5. Thomas Wright, *St. Patrick's Purgatory; an Essay on the Legends of Purgatory, Hell, and Paradise Current During the Middle Ages* (London: John Russell Smith, 1904), 10–13.

6. Ibid., 10–11.

7. St. John D. Seymour, *Irish Visions of the Other World: A Contribution to the Study of Medieval Visions* (London: Society for Promoting Christian Knowledge, 1930; reprint Xerox University Microfilms, 1975), 179.

8. Easting, "Owein," 166.

9. Wright, "St. Patrick's," 60–61.

10. Seymour, *Irish Visions,* 178.

11. Wright, "St. Patrick's," 135.

12. Frances A. Foster, "Legends of the After-Life," in *A Manual of the Writings in Middle English,* ed. J. Burke Severs (Conn.: Academy of Arts and Sciences, 1970), 2: 453–54.

13. Mabel A. Stanford, "The Sumner's Tale and Saint Patrick's Purgatory," *The Journal of English and Germanic Philology* 19 (1920): 380–81.

14. Seymour, *Irish Visions* 181–82.

15. Ibid., 183–85.

16. Ibid., 186.

17. Ibid., 179. The Middle English text says the Owain was a knight of King Stephen, and the English king of that name is the only one known. However, this is probably an error, according to Easting ("Owein" 164–65), who traces the confusion back to the author, Henry of Sawtrey, who "mentions Stephen once only . . . in order to give an approximate date for Owein's visit" (165). Easting suggests that the chronicler Roger of Wendover may have amended the tale to "have Owein serve under Stephen . . . to explain Owein's hypothetical knowledge of English" (164).

18. Seymour, *Irish Visions,* 186.

19. Easting, "Owein," 159–60.

20. Wright, "St. Patrick's," 140.

21. Foster, "Legends of the After-Life," 455.

22. Ibid., 454.

23. Brother Marcus, *The Vision of Tnugdal,* trans. Jean-Michel Picard, introduction by Yolande de Pontfarcy (Dublin: Four Courts Press, 1989). Pontfarcy argues that Brother Marcus's Otherworld corresponds in many ways with his native Ireland.

> It is a real place, the structure of which reflects the same intricacy as the structure of this world, that is to say—as far as Marcus was concerned—Ireland or Munster. . . . One must remember that Ireland was and still is divided into four provinces. . . . These four great provinces and the centre constituted the ordered cosmos. (65)

24. Mearns, *Vision of Tundale,* 7.

25. Ibid.

26. Ibid., 10.

27. Ibid., 9.

28. Ibid., 60–61.

29. Ibid., 61.

30. Ibid., 68.

31. Ibid., 11.

32. Ibid., 24.

33. See Mearns, *Vision of Tundale,* 36–37 for details of the Irish sevenfold

scheme of Heaven and its surrounding zones, possibly to be identified with Purgatory.

34. Ibid., 31–34.

35. Ibid., 32–36.

36. Ibid., 35–36.

37. Ibid., 40. Oddly enough, the Latin text reads "Sanctus Brandanus"; Mearns makes no comment on this. Perhaps a scribal misreading?

38. Ibid., 42.

39. Ibid.

40. Ibid.

41. Ibid., 8, 42.

42. G. R. Owst, *Literature and Pulpit in Medieval England,* 2d rev. ed. (Oxford: Blackwell, 1961), 173.

43. Ibid.

44. Siegfried Wenzel, letter to the author, 13 June 1987.

45. John Mirk, *Mirk's Festial: A Collection of Homilies,* ed. Theodor Erbe, part 1, EETS, e.s., no. 96 (London: K. Paul, Trench, Trübner and Co., 1905). Subsequent quotations from this work are cited parenthetically in the text.

46. James Yonge, "The Gouernance of Princes," in *Secreta Secretorum: The Gouernance of Kynges and Prynces; Three Prose Versions,* ed. Robert Steele, EETS, o.s., no. 74 (London: 1898).

47. *The Dicts and Sayings of the Philosophers,* ed. Curt F. Bühler, EETS, o.s., no. 211 (London: Oxford University Press, 1941). Subsequent quotations from this work are cited parenthetically in the text.

48. Quoted in Alan J. Fletcher, "John Mirk and the Lollards," *Medium Ævum* 56, no. 2 (1982): 217.

49. Ibid., 217.

50. Susan Powell, "A New Dating of John Mirk's *Festial,*" *Notes and Queries* 227, no. 6 (1982): 487–89. Fletcher argues that the date may be further defined to between 1382 and 1390, "probably at the latter end of those years, on the grounds that Mirk knew something of the activities of the Lollards" (218).

51. Mirk was evidently acquainted with Higden's *Polychronicon,* since he cites that source for at least one exemplum: "Rondylf Hyldon, monke of Chestyr, tellyþe yn hys cronyclys anoþyr myracull. . . ." (81). This suggests that he could have also read the derogatory description of the Irish which Higden took from Giraldus.

52. Powell, "New Dating," 388.

53. *The Owl and the Nightingale,* ed. E. G. Stanley (London: Thomas Nelson and Sons, 1960); William Langland, *Piers Plowman: The B Version,* eds. George Kane and E. Talbot Donaldson (London: Athlone Press, 1975). Subsequent quotations from these works are cited parenthetically in the text.

54. Stanley, *Owl and the Nightingale,* n. 113.

55. Kathryn Huganir, *The Owl and the Nightingale: Sources, Date, Author* (Philadelphia: University of Pennsylvania Press, 1931), 99.

56. The owl's words here are based on the "common knowledge" of the time (Stanley, n. 125) that nightingales do not frequent some countries. Huganir notes that Giraldus Cambrensis stated in *Topographia Hibernica* that there are no nightingales in Ireland (99).

57. Chaucer also mentions the Irish only once. See chapter 2.

58. Curt Bühler, introduction to *The Dicts and Sayings of the Philosophers,* EETS, o.s., no. 211 (London: Oxford University Press, 1941), x–xi.

59. Ibid., xlvii. One of the manuscripts based on Scrope's translation, Manuscript I. 2. 10 Emmanuel College, Cambridge (E), "has quite obviously been in Ireland," on the evidence of a marginal note in Irish (fol. 54b) and other marginal references to Waterford, Cork, and "Richard . . . of bally magrir & tomas skiddy merchantt man & Son of Corck" (Ibid., xxiii).

60. If the translation is correct, I would suspect the passage was added by a Continental translator or scribe, as it seems unlikely that the Arabic original would have included any reference to Ireland at all.

61. "The Middle English Verse Life of St. Edward the Confessor," ed. Grace Edna Moore (Ph.D. diss., University of Pennsylvania, 1942); Margery Kempe, *The Book of Margery Kempe,* eds. Sanford Brown Meech and Hope Emily Allen, EETS, o.s. no. 212 (London: Oxford University Press, 1940). Subsequent quotations from these works are cited parenthetically in the text.

62. Moore, introduction to "Middle English Verse Life," lxviii.

63. Ibid., lxvii.

64. R. M. Wilson, "Three Middle English Mystics," *Essays and Studies by Members of the English Association* 9 (1956): 104.

65. The previously quoted passage from Giraldus concerning Irish deformities is accompanied, in one manuscript, by an illustration of just such a cripple (*History* 16–17, 118).

66. The description of Gilemichel's condition in ll. 533–36, 554–55, suggests strictures as a result of burns received at an early age, rather than a congenital deformity. A similar condition has been documented in epileptic children in Zaïre, who have either fallen into the fire in a seizure, or been deliberately crippled (by burning the backs of their knees) in order to prevent worse damage or, possibly, as part of an attempt to drive out evil spirits (V. Birch Rambo, M.D.).

67. Louise Collis, *Memoirs of a Medieval Woman: The Life of Margery Kempe* (New York: Thomas Y. Crowell, 1964), 118.

68. Wilson, "Middle English Mystics," 111. However, Karma Lochrie has questioned Wilson's (and others') definition of "influence" and calls for a reevaluation of Kempe's influence in light of manuscript evidence, and the works of at least one later writer who had read her. (Karma Lochrie, *Margary Kempe and Translations of the Flesh* [Philadelphia: University of Pennsylvania Press, 1991], 8, 202–28.)

Chapter 6. Conclusions

1. Giraldus, *History,* 112–17; Watt, *Church,* 72 passim.

2. V. H. Galbraith, "Roger of Wendover and Matthew Paris," *Kings and Chroniclers: Essays in English Medieval History* (London: The Hambledon Press, 1982), X:6.

3. Morton W. Bloomfield, "History *and* Literature in the Vernacular in the Middle Ages?" in *Medieval English Studies Presented to George Kane,* eds. Edward Donald Kennedy, Ronald Waldron, and Joseph S. Wittig (Wolfeboro, N.H.: D.S. Brewer, 1988), 314.

4. Derek Pearsall, "Middle English Romance and Its Audiences," in *Historical and Editorial Studies in Medieval and Early Modern English,* eds. Mary-Jo Arn and Hanneke Wirtjes, with Hans Jensen (Groningen, The Netherlands: Wolters-Nordhoff, 1985), 42.

5. Karl Brunner, "Middle English Metrical Romances and Their Audience,"

in *Studies in Medieval Literature,* ed. MacEdward Leach (Philadelphia: University of Pennsylvania Press, 1961), 225.

6. Jörg O. Fichte, "The Middle English Arthurian Romance: The Popular Tradition in the Fourteenth Century," in *Literature in Fourteenth-Century England,* eds. Piero Boitani and Anna Torti (1983), 139.

7. Jutta Wurster, "The Audience," in *The Alliterative Morte Arthure: A Reassessment of the Poem,* ed. Karl Heinz Göller (Cambridge, U.K.: D.S. Brewer, 1981), 47.

8. Stephen Knight, "The Social Function of the Middle English Romances," in *Medieval Literature: Criticism, Ideology and History,* ed. David Aers (Brighton, U.K.: The Harvester Press, 1986), 101, 119.

9. Louis Gougaud, *Les Saints irlandais hors d'Irlande: Etudiés dans le culte et dans la dévotion traditionelle,* Bibliothèque de la Révue d'Histoire Ecclésiastique (Oxford: Blackwell, 1936), 1–3, 65–66.

10. John Hennig, "The Place of Irish Saints in Late Mediaeval English Hagiography," *Medieval Studies* 16 (1954): 165, 167; "The Place of Irish Saints in Medieval English Calendars," *The Irish Ecclesiastical Record,* 5th ser., August 1954: 101–3.

11. A. J. Otway-Ruthven, *A History of Medieval Ireland,* 2d ed. (1967; London: Ernest Benn, 1980), 291–92.

12. Knight, "Social Function," 101.

13. Pearsall, "Middle English Romance," 42–43; D. W. Robertson, Jr., "Who Were 'The People'?" in *The Popular Literature of Medieval England,* ed. Thomas J. Heffernan, Tennessee Studies in Literature (Knoxville: University of Tennessee Press, 1985), 28:17.

14. Robertson, "Who Were 'the People'?"

15. Wurster, "Audience," 49.

16. Wurster goes on to say that in spite of the prevalence of English, "French books on secular subjects outnumbered their English counterparts by far" during this time, which, she says, "suggests that members of the nobility were not among the owners of literary manuscripts in English" (49–50). I think it suggests only that French was "fashionable" among the aristocracy, and that they had more money to buy or commission books. Probably the majority of those who would buy or read manuscripts in English would have been among the rising merchant class (Robertson, Who Were 'the People'?" 11, 16–17). However, this French literature is not at all irrelevant; for example, it seems that evidence of aristocratic views of Ireland and the Irish is to be found in the fourteenth-century works of Froissart; see A. H. Diverres, "The Irish Adventures in Froissart's *Meliador,*" Publications Romanes et Françaises 112, *Mélanges de Langue et de Littérature du Moyen Age et de la Renaissance, Offerts à Jean Frappier* (Geneva: Librarie Droz, 1970), 235–51. Concerning Froissart, Robertson writes, "We sometimes forget that the *Chronicles* of Froissart were at one time 'popular' reading for boys throughout England and that men with military experience or aspirations were likely to have been even more interested in them earlier" (21).

17. Otway-Ruthven, *Medieval Ireland,* 102.

18. David Beers Quin, *The Elizabethans and the Irish* (Ithaca, N.Y.: Cornell University Press, 1966), 8.

19. Ibid., 8.

20. Steven G. Ellis, *Reform and Revival: English Government in Ireland, 1470–1534* (New York: St. Martin's Press, 1986), 9.

21. Denis Bethell, "English Monks and Irish Reform in the Eleventh and

Twelfth Centuries," *Historical Studies* 8. Papers read before the Irish Conference of Historians, 27–30 May 1969 (Dublin: Gill and Macmillan, 1971), 128.

22. However, the idea of Ireland as *"insula barbarorum"* is found in Latin as early as 1156 (ibid., 126).

23. Quoted in ibid., 125.

24. Quoted in Marie Therese Flanagan, *Irish Society, Anglo-Norman Settlers, Angevin Kingship: Interactions in Ireland in the Late Twelfth Century* (Oxford: Clarendon Press, 1989), 49.

25. Walter Ullmann, "On the Influence of Geoffrey of Monmouth in English History," in *Speculum Historiale,* ed. C. Bauer, L. Boehm, and M. Müller (Freiburg: Alber, 1965), 268.

26. Again, Giraldus is the obvious example (*History* 106, 112–16; cf. *Polychronicon* I.377–81), though anti-Irish feeling was not confined to Anglo-Norman or English clerics. Major figures in the Irish church reform movement of the twelfth century, such as St. Malachy, spoke strongly against abuses by their fellow countrymen (J.A. Watt, *The Church and the Two Nations in Medieval Ireland* [New York: Cambridge University Press, 1970], 19–20), and the Irish bishops were among the first to accept the lordship of Henry II (ibid., 39–40). The most notable example of anti-Irish sentiments refers to English and Hiberno-English clerics in Ireland; that is, the oft-cited passage from the fourteenth-century "Remonstrance of the Irish Princes" sent to the pope, protesting that

> not only [English] laymen and secular clergy but also some of their regular clergy dogmatically assert the heresy that it is no more a sin to kill an Irishman than a dog. . . . And in maintaining this heresy some of their monks boldly assert . . . that when, as often happens, they kill an Irishman, they do not on that account refrain from saying mass, even for a day. (quoted in Watt, *Church,* 188)

27. Art Cosgrove, "England and Ireland, 1399–1449," in *Medieval Ireland 1169–1534,* vol. 2 of *A New History of Ireland,* ed. Cosgrove (Oxford: Clarendon Press, 1987), 528–29.

28. Bernard Bailyn et al., *The Great Republic: A History of the American People,* 2d ed. (Lexington, Mass.: D.C. Heath, 1981), 1:24.

29. Quin, *Elizabethans,* 23–27.

30. Flanagan, *Irish Society,* 57–68.

31. On the other hand, the young St. Cuthbert and his mother went into exile from Ireland to England.

32. H. R. Patch, *The Other World According to Descriptions in Medieval Literature,* Smith College Studies in Modern Languages, new series, 1 (Cambridge, Mass.: 1950), 25–59.

33. Flanagan, *Irish Society,* 68–69.

34. T. Mcalindon, "The Treatment of the Supernatural in Middle English Legend and Romance, 1200–1400" (Ph.D. diss., Fitzwilliam House, Cambridge University, 1961), 108.

35. Joseph Dunn, "The Brendan Problem," *The Catholic Historical Review* 6, no. 4 (1921), 465–67.

36. Carl Selmer, ed., introduction to Navigatio Sancti Brendani Abbatis *from Early Latin Manuscripts* (Notre Dame, Inc.: University of Notre Dame Press, 1959), xxvii, xxxi; Dunn, "Brendan Problem," 468.

37. Felim Ó Brian, "Saga Themes in Irish Hagiography," in *Féilscríbhinn Torna: Essays and Studies Presented to Professor Tadhg Ua Donnchada (Torna),* ed. Séamus Pender (Dublin: Cork University Press, 1947).

38. Diverres, "Irish Adventures," 249.
39. Ibid., 248–49.
40. Otway-Ruthven, *History,* 291–94.
41. Edward D. Snyder, "The Wild Irish: A Study of Some English Satires Against the Irish, Scots, and Welsh," *Modern Philology* 17 (1920): 154–57; Quin, *Elizabethans and Irish,* 2–6.

Bibliography

Primary Sources

[*Alliterative Morte Arthure.*] *Morte Arthure, or The Death of Arthur.* Edited by Edmund Brock. Early English Text Society (EETS), original series (o.s.), no. 8. London: K. Paul, Trench, Trübner, 1871; rpt. 1904.

An Alphabet of Tales. Edited by Mary McLeod Banks. EETS, o.s., 126–27. London: K. Paul, Trench, Trübner and Co., 1904–5.

The Anglo-Saxon Chronicle: A Revised Translation. Edited and translated by Dorothy Whitelock. New Brunswick, N.J.: Rutgers University Press, 1961.

[*Arthoure and Merlin.*] *Of Arthoure and of Merlin.* Edited by O. D. Macrae-Gibson. 2 vols. EETS, o.s., nos. 268, 279. New York: Oxford University Press, 1973, 1979.

Bede's Ecclesiastical History of the English People [*Historia Ecclesiastica Gentis Anglorum*]. Edited and translated by Bertram Colgrave and R. A. B. Mynors. Oxford: Oxford University Press, 1969.

"Cambrai Homily." *Thesaurus Palaeohibernicus.* Vol. 2. Edited by Whitley Stokes. Dublin: Dublin Institute for Advanced Studies, 1975. 244–47.

Capgrave, John. *Capgrave's Abbreuiacion of Cronicles.* Edited by Peter J. Lucas. EETS, o.s., no. 285. New York: Oxford University Press, 1983.

Caxton, William. *Caxton's Mirrour of the World.* Edited by Oliver H. Prior. EETS, extra series (e.s.), no. 110. New York: Oxford University Press, 1966.

Chaucer, Geoffrey. "The Romaunt of the Rose." In *The Works of Geoffrey Chaucer.* 2d ed. Edited F. N. Robinson. Boston: Houghton Mifflin, 1957.

Chestre, Thomas. *Sir Launfal.* Edited by A. J. Bliss. London: Thomas Nelson and Sons, 1960.

The Dicts and Sayings of the Philosophers. Edited by Curt F. Bühler. EETS, o.s., no. 211. London: Oxford University Press, 1941.

The Early South English Legendary, or Lives of Saints. Edited by Carl Horstmann. EETS, o.s., no. 87. London: 1887.

The English Conquest of Ireland. Edited by F. J. Furnivall. EETS, o.s., no. 107. London: 1896.

"A Fifteenth-Century Prose Paraphrase of Robert of Gloucester's Chronicle." Edited by Andrew D. Lipscomb. Ph.D. diss., University of North Carolina at Chapel Hill, 1990.

Geoffrey of Monmouth. *The History of the Kings of Britain* [*Historia Regum Britanniae*]. Translated and edited by Lewis Thorpe. 1966. New York: Viking Penguin Inc., 1986.

Gerald of Wales [Giraldus Cambrensis]. *The History and Topography of Ireland.*

[*Historia et Topographia Hibernica*]. Translated by John J. O'Meara. 1951. New York: Penguin Books, 1982.

Gildas. *The Ruin of Britain and Other Works* [*De Excidio Britanniae*]. Edited and translated Michael Winterbottom. History from the Sources. Totowa, N.J.: Rowman and Littlefield, 1978.

Giraldus Cambrensis. *Expugnatio Hibernica* [*The Conquest of Ireland*]. Edited and translated by A. B. Scott and F. X. Martin. Dublin: Royal Irish Academy, 1978.

―――. *Historia et Topographia Hibernica*. Edited by J. S. Brewer. *Giraldi Cambrensis Opera*, vol. 5. London: 1861–91.

"Horn Childe." *King Horn: A Middle English Romance*. Edited by Joseph Hall. Oxford: Clarendon Press, 1901.

Horn Childe and Maiden Rimnild. Edited by Maldwyn Mills. Middle English Texts 20. Heidelberg: Carl Winter, 1988.

"A Hymn to Mary." *Early English Lyrics: Amorous, Divine, Moral, and Trivial*. Edited by E. K. Chambers and F. Sidgwick. London: Sidgwick and Jackson Ltd., 1966. 97–99.

"Ich am of Irlaunde." Edited by John Speirs. *Medieval English Poetry: The Non-Chaucerian Tradition*. London: Faber and Faber, 1957. 60–61.

Kempe Margery. *The Book of Margery Kempe*. Edited by Sanford Brown Meech and Hope Emily Allen. EETS, o.s., no. 212. London: Oxford University Press, 1940.

King Horn. Edited by Rosamund Allen. Garland Medieval Texts 7. New York and London: Garland Publishing, 1984.

"The Land of Cokaygne." *Early Middle English Verse and Prose*. Edited by J. A. W. Bennett and G. V. Smithers. 2d ed. Oxford: Clarendon Press, 1968. 136–44.

Langland, William. *Piers Plowman: The B Version*. Edited by George Kane and E. Talbot Donaldson. London: Athlone Press, 1975.

Laȝamon. *Brut*. Edited by G. L. Brook and R. F. Leslie. 2 vols. EETS, o.s., 250, 277. New York: Oxford University Press, 1963, 1978.

"The libelle of Englysshe polycye." *Political Poems and Songs Relating to English Antiquity*. Vol. 2. Edited by Thomas Wright. Rolls Series 14. London: 1859–61.

Liber Exemplorum ad Usum Praedicantium: Saeculo XIII compositus a quodam Fratre Minore Anglico de provincia Hiberniae. Edited by A. G. Little. Aberdeen: Typis Academicis, 1980.

The Life of St. Cuthbert in English Verse, c. A.D. 1450, from the original MS in the library at Castle Howard. Edited by J. T. Fowler. Surtees Society 87. Edinburgh: 1891.

Louelich, Henry, trans. *The History of the Holy Grail*. Edited by F. J. Furnivall. EETS, e.s., no. 30 (pt. 4). London: 1878.

―――. *Merlin*. Edited by Ernst A. Kock. 5 Parts. EETS, e.s. 93, 105, 112. London: K. Paul, Trench, Trübner, 1904–13. EETS, o.s. 112, 185. London: 1899; rpt. H. Milford, Oxford University Press, 1932.

Lybeaus Desconus. Edited by M. Mills. EETS, o.s., no. 261. London: Oxford University Press, 1969.

Lydgate John. *The Sudden Fall of Princes*. In *Historical Poems of the XIVth and XVth Centuries*. Edited by Rossell Hope Robbins. New York: Columbia University Press, 1959.

Malory, Thomas. "Balin or the Knight With the Two Swords." *Works.* 2d ed. Edited by Eugène Vinaver. New York: Oxford University Press, 1978; rpt. 1981.

——. "The Book of Sir Tristram de Lyones." *Works.* 2d ed. Edited by Eugène Vinaver. New York: Oxford University Press, 1978; rpt. 1981.

The Macro Plays. Edited by Mark Eccles. EETS, o.s. 262. London, New York: Oxford University Press, 1969.

"Mankind." *The Macro Plays.* Edited by F. J. Furnivall and Alfred W. Pollard. EETS, e.s., no. 91. London: K. Paul, Trench, Trübner, 1904.

Mannyng, Robert, of Brunne. *Robert of Brunne's Handlyng Synne and Its French Original.* Edited by F.J. Furnivall. EETS, o.s., nos. 119, 123. 1901–3; rpt. Millwood, N.Y.: Kraus Reprint Co., 1975, 1976.

——. *The Story of England.* 2 vols. Edited by F. J. Furnivall. Rolls Series, no. 87. London: 1887.

Marcus, Brother. *The Vision of Tnugdal.* Translated by Jean-Michel Picard, introduction by Yolande de Pontfarcy. Dublin: Four Courts Press, 1989.

Memorials of St. Dunstan. Edited by William Stubbs. Rolls Series 63. London: 1874.

"The Middle English Verse Life of St. Edward the Confessor." Edited by Grace Edna Moore. Ph.D. diss., University of Pennsylvania, 1942.

Mirk, John. *Mirk's Festial: A Collection of Homilies.* Edited by Theodor Erbe. Part 1. EETS, e.s., no. 96. London: K. Paul, Trench, Trübner and Co., 1905.

Mum and the Sothsegger. Edited by Mabel Day and Robert Steele. EETS, o.s., no. 199. London: H. Milford for Oxford University Press, 1936.

Nennius. *British History and The Welsh Annals [Historia Brittonum et Annales Cambriae].* Edited and translated by John Morris. History from the Sources. Totowa, N.J.: Rowman and Littlefield, 1980.

"On the Minorites." *Historical Poems of the XIVth and XVth Centuries.* Edited by Rossell Hope Robbins. New York: Columbia University Press, 1959.

The Owl and the Nightingale. Edited by E. G. Stanley. London: Thomas Nelson and Sons Ltd., 1960.

Paris, Matthew. *Chronica Maiora.* Edited by Henry Richards Luard. Rolls series 57 (7 vols.) London: 1872–83.

——. *Chronicles of Matthew Paris: Monastic Life in the Thirteenth Century.* Edited and translated by Robert Vaughan. Gloucester, England: A. Sutton; New York: St. Martin's Press, 1984.

[Prose Brut] The Brut, or The Chronicles of England. Edited by Friedrich W. D. Brie. 2 vols. EETS, o.s., 131, 136. London: K. Paul Trench, Trübner & Co., 1906, 1908.

[Prose Merlin.] Merlin, or The Early History of King Arthur. Edited by Henry B. Wheatley. EETS, o.s., nos. 10, 21. London: 1865, 1877.

Richard the Redeless. Edited by W. Skeat. EETS, o.s., no. 54. London: 1873.

Robert of Gloucester. *The Metrical Chronicle of Robert of Gloucester.* 2 vols. Edited by William A. Wright. London: 1887.

The Romance of Guy of Warwick. Part 2. Edited by Julius Zupitza. EETS, e.s., no. 49. London: 1887.

The Romans of Partenay, or of Lusignan. Edited by W. Skeat. EETS, o.s., no. 22. London: K. Paul, Trench, Trübner, 1866; rev. and rpt. 1899.

"The Siege of Calais." *Historical Poems of the XIVth and XVth Centuries.* Edited by Rossell Hope Robbins. New York: Columbia University Press, 1959.

Sir Tristrem. Edited by George P. McNeill. Scottish Text Society 8. 1886; rpt. New York: Johnson Reprint Corp., 1966.

The South English Legendary. Edited by Charlotte D'Evelyn and Arna J. Mill. Vol. 1. EETS, o.s., no. 235. London: Oxford University Press, 1956.

[*Stanzaic Morte Arthure*] *Le Morte Arthure.* Edited by J. Douglas Bruce. EETS, e.s., no. 88. 1903; rpt. New York: AMS Press, 1979.

Trevisa, John, tr. *Polychronicon Ranulphi Higden.* Rolls Series 14 (9 vols.). Vol. 1. Edited by Churchill Babington. London: 1865. Vols. 5, 6. Edited by Joseph Rawson Lumby. London: 1874, 1876.

"The Twelve Letters to Save Merry England." *Political, Religious, and Love Poems.* Edited by F.J. Furnivall. EETS., o.s., no. 15. London: K. Paul, Trench, Trübner, 1866; reedited, 1903.

Two of the Saxon Chronicles Parallel. Revised and edited by Charles Plummer. Oxford: Clarendon Press, 1892.

The Vision of Tundale. Edited by Rodney Mearns. Middle English Texts 18. Heidelberg: Carl Winter, 1985.

William of Malmesbury. *Chronicle of the Kings of England* [*De Gestis Regum Anglorum*]. Edited by J. A. Giles. London: George Bell and Sons, 1904.

Yonge, James. "The Gouernance of Princes." Edited by Robert Steele. *Secreta Secretorum: The Gouernance of Kynges and Prynces; Three Prose Versions.* EETS, e.s. 74. London: K. Paul, Trench, Trübner, 1898.

Secondary Sources

Bailyn, Bernard, Robert Dallek, David Brion Davis, David Herbert Donald, John Thomas, and Gordon Wood. *The Great Republic: A History of the American People.* 2d ed. Vol. I. Lexington, Mass.: D.C. Heath and Company, 1981.

Bergin, Osborn. "White Red-Eared Cows." *Ériu* 14, part 2 (1946): 170.

Bethell, Denis. "English Monks and Irish Reform in the Eleventh and Twelfth Centuries." *Historical Studies* 8. Papers read before the Irish Conference of Historians, 27–30 May 1969. Dublin: Gill and Macmillan, 1971. 111–35.

Binchy, D. A. "Patrick and His Biographers: Ancient and Modern." *Studia Hibernica* 2 (1962): 7–173.

Bloomfield, Morton W. "History *and* Literature in the Vernacular in the Middle Ages?" In *Medieval English Studies Presented to George Kane.* Edited by Edward Donald Kennedy, Ronald Waldron, and Joseph S. Wittig. Wolfeboro, N.H.: D.S. Brewer, 1988. 309–15.

Bowen, E. G. "The Cult of St. Brigit." *Studia Celtica* 8–9 (1973–74): 33–47.

Boyd, Beverly. "A New Approach to the *South English Legendary.*" *Philological Quarterly* 47 (1968): 494–98.

Braswell, Mary Flowers. *The Medieval Sinner: Characterization and Confession in the Literature of the English Middle Ages.* Rutherford, N.J.: Fairleigh Dickinson Press; London: Associated University Presses, 1983.

Brunner, Karl. "Middle English Metrical Romances and Their Audience." In

Studies in Medieval Literature. Edited by MacEdward Leach. Philadelphia: University of Pennsylvania Press, 1961. 219–27.

Burrow, J. A. "The Audience of Piers Plowman." In *Essays on Medieval Literature.* Oxford: Clarendon Press, 1984.

———. *Medieval Writers and Their Work: Middle English Literature and Its Background 1100–1500.* Oxford: Oxford University Press, 1982.

———. "Poems Without Contexts: The Rawlinson ·Lyrics." In *Essays on Medieval Literature.* Oxford: Clarendon Press, 1984. 1–26.

———. "Postscript." *Essays on Medieval Literature.* Oxford: Clarendon Press, 1984.

Bzdyl, Donald G., trans. *Layamon's* Brut: *A History of the Britons.* Medieval and Renaissance Texts and Studies, vol. 65. Binghamton, N.Y.: Medieval & Renaissance Texts and Studies, 1989.

Calendar of Documents Relating to Ireland. 1171–1307. H.M. Public Record Office. Edited by H. S. Sweetman. London: 1875–86.

Caluwé-Dor, Juliette de. "L'Elément Irlandais dans la version moyen-anglais de *The Land of Cockaygne.*" In *Mélanges de Langue et Littérature Françaises du Moyen Age et de la Renaissance offerts à Charles Foulon.* vol. 1. Rennes, France: Institut de Français, Université de Haute-Bretagne, 1980. 89–98.

Coleman, Janet. *Medieval Readers and Writers: 1350–1400.* New York: Columbia University Press, 1981.

Colgrave, Bertram, ed. *Two Lives of St. Cuthbert: A Life by an Anonymous Monk of Lindisfarne and Bede's Prose Life.* Cambridge, U.K.: The University Press, 1940.

Collis, Louise. *Memoirs of a Medieval Woman: The Life of Margery Kempe.* New York: Thomas Y. Crowell, 1964.

Cosgrove, Art. "England and Ireland, 1399–1449." In *Medieval Ireland 1169–1534.* Vol. 2 of *A New History of Ireland.* Edited by Art Cosgrove. Oxford: Clarendon Press, 1987.

Craster, H.H.E. "The Red Book of Durham." *The English Historical Review* 40 (1925): 504–32.

Curtis, Edmund. *A History of Medieval Ireland from 1086–1513.* 1938; rpt. London: Methuen and Co. Ltd., 1978.

Curtius, Ernst Robert. *European Literature and the Latin Middle Ages.* Translated by Willard R. Trask. London: Routledge and K. Paul, 1953.

D'Evelyn, Charlotte and Frances A. Foster. "Saints' Legends." In *A Manual of the Writings in Middle English.* vol. 2. Edited by J. Burke Severs. Connecticut: Academy of Arts and Sciences, 1970. 410–57.

Diverres, A. H. "The Irish Adventures in Froissart's *Meliador.*" Publications Romanes et Françaises 112. In *Mélanges de Langue et de Littérature du Moyen Age et de la Renaissance, Offerts à Jean Frappier.* Geneva: Librarie Droz, 1970. 235–51.

Dodds, Madeleine Hope, trans. and ed. "The Little Book of the Birth of St. Cuthbert, Commonly Called the Irish Life of St. Cuthbert." *Archaeologica Aeliana: or, Miscellaneous Tracts Relating to Antiquity.* 4th ser. 6 (1929): 52–94.

Dolley, Michael. *Anglo-Norman Ireland, c. 1100–1318.* Dublin: Gill and Macmillan Ltd., 1972.

Down, Kevin. "Colonial Society and Economy in the High Middle Ages." *Medie-*

val Ireland 1169–1534. Vol. 2 of *A New History of Ireland.* Edited by Art Cosgrove. Oxford: Clarendon Press, 1987. 439–91.

Dunn, Joseph. "The Brendan Problem." *The Catholic Historical Review* 6, no. 4 (1921): 395–477.

Easting, Robert. "The Date and Dedication of the *Tractatus de Purgatorio Sancti Patricii.*" *Speculum* 53 (1978): 778–83.

———. "Owein at St. Patrick's Purgatory." *Medium Ævum* 55, no. 2 (1986): 159–75.

———. "Peter of Cornwall's Account of St. Patrick's Purgatory." *Analecta Bollandiana* 97 (1979): 397–416.

Ellis, Steven G. *Reform and Revival: English Government in Ireland, 1470–1534.* New York: St. Martin's Press, 1986.

Eyre, Charles. *The History of St. Cuthbert.* 3d ed. New York: 1887.

Fichte, Jörg O. "The Middle English Arthurian Romance: The Popular Tradition in the Fourteenth Century." In *Literature in Fourteenth-Century England.* Edited by Piero Boitani and Anna Torti. 1983. 137–53.

FitzMaurice, E. B. and A. G. Little, eds. *Materials for the History of the Franciscan Province of Ireland, A.D. 1230–1450.* Manchester: The University Press, 1920.

Flanagan, Marie Therese. *Irish Society, Anglo-Norman Settlers, Angevin Kingship: Interactions in Ireland in the Late Twelfth Century.* Oxford: Clarendon Press, 1989.

Fletcher, Alan J. "John Mirk and the Lollards." *Medium Ævum* 56, no. 2 (1982): 216–24.

Fletcher, Robert Huntington. *The Arthurian Material in the Chronicles.* 2d ed. New York: Burt Franklin, 1966; rpt. Lenox Hill, 1973.

Foster, Frances A. "Legends of the After-Life." In *A Manual of the Writings in Middle English,* vol. 2. Edited by J. Burke Severs. Connecticut: Academy of Arts and Sciences, 1970. 452–56.

Fowler, J. T., ed. *The Life of St. Cuthbert in English Verse, c. A.D. 1450, from the original MS in the library at Castle Howard.* Surtees Society 87. Edinburgh: 1891.

Frame, Robin. *Colonial Ireland, 1169–1369.* Helicon History of Ireland. Dublin: Helicon, 1981.

French, Walter H. *Essays on King Horn.* Cornell Studies in English 30. Ithaca, N.Y.: Cornell University Press, 1940.

Galbraith, V. H. "Historical Research in Medieval England." *Kings and Chroniclers: Essays in English Medieval History.* London: The Hambledon Press, 1982. 11:1–46.

———. "Roger of Wendover and Matthew Paris." In *Kings and Chroniclers: Essays in English Medieval History.* London: The Hambledon Press, 1982. 10: 5–48.

Garbáty, Thomas Jay. "Studies in the Franciscan 'The Land of Cokaygne' in the Kildare MS." *Franziskanische Studien* 45 (1963): 139–53.

Gardiner, Eileen. "A Solution to the Problem of Dating in the *Vision of Tundale.*" *Medium Ævum* 51 (1982): 86–91.

Glasscock, R. E. "Land and People, c. 1300." In *Medieval Ireland 1169–1534.*

vol. 2 of *A New History of Ireland.* Edited by Art Cosgrove. Oxford: Clarendon Press, 1987.

Göller, Karl Heinz. "Reality versus Romance: A Reassessment of the *Alliterative Morte Arthure.*" In *The* Alliterative Morte Arthure: *A Reassessment of the Poem.* Edited by Karl Heinz Göller. Cambridge, U.K.: D.S. Brewer 1981. 15–29.

Gougaud, Louis. *Les Saints irlandais hors d'Irlande: Etudiés dans le culte et dans la dévotion traditionelle.* Bibliothèque de la Révue d'Histoire Ecclésiastique. Oxford: Blackwell, 1936.

Greene, Richard Leighton. *The Early English Carols.* Oxford: Clarendon Press, 1935.

Hall, D. J. *English Medieval Pilgrimage.* London: Routledge and Kegan Paul, 1965.

Hamel, Mary. *Morte Arthure: A Critical Edition [Alliterative Morte Arthure].* Garland Medieval Texts 9. New York: Garland Publishing, 1984.

Hennig, John. "Ireland's Place in the Tradition of the Cistercian Menology." *Irish Ecclesiastical Record* 95 (1961): 306–17.

———. "The Place of Irish Saints in Late Mediaeval English Hagiography." *Medieval Studies* 16 (1954): 165–71.

———. "The Place of Irish Saints in Mediaeval English Calendars." *The Irish Ecclesiastical Record.* 5th ser. August 1954: 93–106.

Henry, P. L. "The Land of Cokaygne: Cultures in Contact in Medieval Ireland." *Studia Hibernica* 12 (1972): 120–41.

Heuser, W. *Die Kildare-Gedichte: Die Ältesten Mittelenglishen Denkmäler in Anglo-Irischer Überlieferung.* Darmstadt: Wissenschaftliche Buchgesellschaft, 1965 (reprint).

Holland, Norman. "Ich am of Irlaunde." *Explicator* 15, no. 9 (1957): item 55.

Howard, Donald R. *Chaucer: His Life, His Works, His World.* New York: E.P. Dutton, 1987.

Huganir, Kathryn. *The Owl and the Nightingale: Sources, Date, Author.* Philadelphia: University of Pennsylvania Press, 1931.

Hughes, Kathleen. *The Church in Early Irish Society.* Ithaca, N.Y.: Cornell University Press, 1966.

Jones, W. R. "The Image of the Barbarian in Medieval Europe." *Comparative Studies in Society and History* 13, no. 4 (October 1971): 376–407.

Kennedy, Edward Donald. *Chronicles and Other Historical Writings.* Vol. 8 of *A Manual of the Writings in Middle English 1050–1500.* Edited by Albert E. Hartung. New Haven, Conn.: Archon Books, 1989.

Kenney, James F. "The Legend of St. Brendan." *Proceedings and Transactions of the Royal Society of Canada.* 3d ser. 14 (1920): 51–67.

———. *The Sources for the Early History of Ireland,* Vol. 1: *Ecclesiastical.* 1929. Revised by Ludwig Bieler, 1966; rpt. Dublin: Pádraic Ó Táilliúir, 1979.

Ker, Neil R. *English Manuscripts in the Century After the Norman Conquest.* Oxford: Clarendon Press, 1960.

Knight, Stephen. "The Social Function of the Middle English Romances." In *Medieval Literature: Criticism, Ideology and History.* Edited by David Aers. Brighton, U.K.: The Harvester Press, 1986. 99–122.

Krishna, Valerie, ed. *The Alliterative Morte Arthure.* New York: Burt Franklin, 1976.

Lane, Darryl F. "An Historical Study of the Giant in the Middle English Metrical Romances." Ph.D. diss., University of New Mexico, 1972.

Lapidge, Michael. "The Cult of St. Indract at Glastonbury." In *Ireland in Early Medieval Europe*. Edited by Dorothy Whitelock, Rosamund McKitterick and David Dumville. New York: Cambridge University Press, 1982.

————, and Richard Sharpe. *A Bibliography of Celtic-Latin Literature, 400–1200*. Dublin: Royal Irish Academy, 1985.

Lavery, Simon. "The Source of the St. Brendan Story in the South English Legendary." *Leeds Studies in English*. New ser. 15 (1984): 21–32.

Lochrie, Karma. *Margery Kempe and Translations of the Flesh*. Philadelphia: University of Pennsylvania Press, 1991.

Lydon, James, ed. *England and Ireland in the Later Middle Ages*. Totowa, N.J.: Irish Academic Press Ltd., 1981.

————. "The Expansion and Consolidation of the Colony, 1215–54." In *Medieval Ireland 1169–1534*. Vol. 2 of *A New History of Ireland*. Edited by Art Cosgrove. Oxford: Clarendon Press, 1987.

————. *Ireland in the Later Middle Ages*. Dublin: Gill and Macmillan, 1973.

————. "The Middle Nation." *The English in Medieval Ireland*. Proceedings of the first joint meeting of the Royal Irish Academy and the British Academy, Dublin, 1982. Edited by James Lydon. Dublin: Royal Irish Academy, 1984.

————. "Richard II's Expeditions to Ireland." *The Journal of the Royal Society of Antiquaries of Ireland* 93, part 2 (1963): 135–49.

Mac Cana, Proinsias. *Branwen Daughter of Llyr*. Cardiff: University of Wales Press, 1958.

Mac Mathúna, Liam. "On the Expression and Concept of Blindness in Irish." *Studia Hibernica* 19 (1979): 26–62.

Mac Niocaill, Gearóid. *Ireland Before the Vikings*. Dublin: Gill and Macmillan, 1972.

Martin, F. X. "Diarmait Mac Murchada and the Coming of the Anglo-Normans." In *Medieval Ireland 1169–1534*. Vol. 2 of *A New History of Ireland*. Edited Art Cosgrove. Oxford: Clarendon Press, 1987.

————. "The Image of the Irish—Medieval and Modern—Continuity and Change." In *Medieval and Modern Ireland*. Edited by Richard Wall. Totowa, N.J.: Barnes and Noble, 1988. 1–18.

McAlindon, T. "The Emergence of a Comic Type in Middle English Narrative: The Devil and Giant as Buffoon." *Anglia* 81 (1962): 365–71.

————. "The Treatment of the Supernatural in Middle English Legend and Romance, 1200–1400." Ph.D. diss., Fitzwilliam House, Cambridge University, 1961.

McKeehan, Irene Pettit. "The Book of the Nativity of St. Cuthbert." *PMLA* 48, no. 4 (1933): 981–99.

————. "Some Relationships Between the Legends of British Saints and the Medieval Romance." *Abstracts of Theses / Humanistic Series*. Chicago: University of Chicago Press, 1926. 383–91.

McNeill, John T. "Perspectives on Celtic Church History." In *Contemporary Reflections on the Medieval Christian Tradition: Essays in Honor of Ray C. Petry*. Edited by George H. Shriver. Durham, N.C.: Duke University Press, n.d.

Ó Brian, Felim, O.F.M. "Saga Themes in Irish Hagiography." In *Féilscríbhinn Torna: Essays and Studies Presented to Professor Tadhg Ua Donnchada (Torna).* Edited by Séamus Pender. Dublin: Cork University Press, 1947.

O'Rahilly, T. F. *Early Irish History and Mythology.* Dublin: Institute for Advanced Studies, 1946.

Orpen, Goddard Henry. *Ireland Under the Normans, 1169–1333.* 4 vols. 1911–20; rpt. Oxford: Clarendon Press, 1968.

Otway-Ruthven, A. J. *A History of Medieval Ireland.* 2d ed. 1967. London: Ernest Benn, 1980.

Owst, G. R. *Literature and Pulpit in Medieval England.* 2d rev. ed. Oxford: Blackwell, 1961.

———. *Preaching in Medieval England: An Introduction to Sermon Manuscripts of the Period c. 1350–1450.* Cambridge, U.K.: The University Press, 1926.

Patch, H. R. "The Adaptation of Otherworld Motifs to Medieval Romance." In *Philologica, the Malone Anniversary Studies.* Edited by Thomas A. Kirby and Henry Bosley Woolf. Baltimore: Johns Hopkins University Press, 1949. 115–23.

———. *The Other World According to Descriptions in Medieval Literature.* Smith College Studies in Modern Languages, new ser. 1. Cambridge, Mass.: 1950.

Pearsall, Derek. "Middle English Romance and Its Audiences." *Historical and Editorial Studies in Medieval and Early Modern English.* Edited by Mary-Jo Arn and Hanneke Wirtjes, with Hans Jensen. Groningen, The Netherlands: Wolters-Nordhoff, 1985.

Peter, John. *Complaint and Satire in Early English Literature.* New York: Oxford University Press, 1955.

Pickering, O.S. "An Early Middle English Verse Inscription from Shrewsbury." *Anglia* 106, nos. 3–4 (1988): 411–14.

Plummer, Charles. "Some New Light on the Brendan Legend." *Zeitschrift für celtische Philologie* 4 (1905): 124–41.

Powell, Susan. "A New Dating of John Mirk's *Festial.*" *Notes and Queries* 227, no. 6 (1982): 487–89.

Quin, David Beers. *The Elizabethans and the Irish.* Ithaca, N.Y.: Cornell University Press, 1966.

Ramsay, Sir James H. *The Angevin Empire; or, The Three Reigns of Henry II, Richard I, and John (A.D. 1154–1216).* New York: Macmillan, 1903; rpt. New York: AMS Press, 1978.

Ransom, James Fitzhugh. "A Study of Henry Louelich's *Merlin.*" *DA* 22: 4345 (Stanford).

Rees, Alwyn, and Brinley Rees. *Celtic Heritage: Ancient Tradition in Ireland and Wales.* 1961; rpt. London: Thames and Hudson, 1989.

Robbins, Rossell Hope, ed. *Historical Poems of the XIVth and XVth Centuries.* New York: Columbia University Press, 1959.

Robertson, D. W., Jr. "Who Were 'The People'?" In *The Popular Literature of Medieval England.* Edited by Thomas J. Heffernan. Tennessee Studies in Literature, vol. 28. Knoxville: University of Tennessee Press, 1985.

Ross, Woodburn O., ed. *Middle English Sermons.* EETS, o.s., 209. London: H. Milford, Oxford University Press, 1940.

Scattergood, V. J. *Politics and Poetry in the Fifteenth Century.* New York: Barnes & Noble, 1972.

Scowcroft, R. Mark. *Leabhar Gabhála,* part 2: The Growth of the Text," *Ériu* 38 (1987): 79–140.

———. *Leabhar Gabhála,* part 2: The Growth of the Tradition." *Ériu* 39 (1988): 1–66.

Selmer, Carl, ed. Navigatio Sancti Brendani Abbatis *from Early Latin Manuscripts.* Notre Dame: University of Notre Dame Press, 1959.

Seymour, St. John D. *Anglo-Irish Literature 1200–1582.* Cambridge, U.K.: The University Press, 1929.

———. *Irish Visions of the Other World: A Contribution to the Study of Medieval Visions.* London: Society for Promoting Christian Knowledge, 1930; rpt. Xerox University Microfilms, 1975.

Slover, Clark H. "Early Literary Channels Between Britain and Ireland." [University of Texas] *Studies in English* 6: 5–52.

———. "Early Literary Channels Between Britain and Ireland." [University of Texas] *Studies in English* 7: 5–111.

———. "William of Malmesbury and the Irish." *Speculum* 2 (1927): 268–83.

———. "William of Malmesbury's *Life of St. Patrick." Modern Philology* 24 (1926): 5–20.

Snyder, E. D. "The Wild Irish: A Study of Some English Satires Against the Irish, Scots, and Welsh." *Modern Philology* 17 (1919–20): 687–725.

Speirs, John. *Medieval English Poetry: The Non-Chaucerian Tradition.* London: Faber and Faber, 1957.

Stanford, Mabel A. "The Sumner's Tale and Saint Patrick's Purgatory." *The Journal of English and Germanic Philology* 19 (1920): 377–81.

Tatlock, J. S. P. "Greater Irish Saints in Lawman and in England." *Modern Philology* 43 (1945–46): 72–76.

———. "Irish Costume in Lawman." *Studies in Philology* 28 (1931): 587–93.

Tupper, Frederick. "Chaucer's Tale of Ireland." *PMLA* 36 (1921): 186–222.

Ullmann, Walter. "On the Influence of Geoffrey of Monmouth in English History." *Speculum Historiale Geschichte im Spiegel von Geschichtsschreibung und Geschichtsdeutung.* Edited by C. Bauer, L. Boehm, and M Müller. Frieburg: Alber, 1965. 257–76.

Watt, J. A. *The Church and the Two Nations in Medieval Ireland.* New York: Cambridge University Press, 1970.

———. "Gaelic Polity and Cultural Identity." In *Medieval Ireland 1169–1534.* Vol. 2 of *A New History of Ireland.* Edited by Art Cosgrove. Oxford: Clarendon Press, 1987.

Wenzel, Seigfried. Letter to the author. 13 June 1987.

———. "Vices, Virtues, and Popular Preaching." In *Medieval and Renaissance Studies.* Proceedings of the South Eastern Institute of Medieval and Renaissance Studies, Summer 1974. Edited by Dale F. J. Randall. 42–45.

Whitelock, Dorothy, Rosamund McKitterick, and David Dumville. *Ireland in Early Medieval Europe.* Cambridge: Cambridge University Press, 1982.

Wilkes, Gerald L. "The Castle of Unite in *Piers Plowman." Medieval Studies* 27 (1965): 334–36.

Willson, Elizabeth. *The Middle English Legends of Visits to the Other World and Their Relations to the Metrical Romances.* Chicago: 1917.

Wilson, R. M. "Three Middle English Mystics." *Essays and Studies by Members of the English Association* 9 (1956): 87–112.

Wright, Thomas. *St. Brandan: A Medieval Legend of the Sea in English Verse and Prose.* Percy Society 14. London: 1844.

———. *St. Patrick's Purgatory; an Essay on the Legends of Purgatory, Hell, and Paradise Current During the Middle Ages.* London: John Russell Smith, 1904.

Wurster, Jutta. "The Audience." *The Alliterative Morte Arthure: A Reassessment of the Poem.* Edited by Karl Heinz Göller. Cambridge: D.S. Brewer, 1981. 44–56.

Index